Citizenship

Citizenship

Citizenship

———

Étienne Balibar

Translated by Thomas Scott-Railton

polity

First published in Italian as *Cittadinanza* © Bollati Boringhieri editore Turin, 2012

This English edition © Polity Press, 2015

Polity Press
65 Bridge Street
Cambridge CB2 1UR, UK

Polity Press
350 Main Street
Malden, MA 02148, USA

ISBN-13: 978-0-7456-8240-2
ISBN-13: 978-0-7456-8241-9 (pb)

A catalogue record for this book is available from the British Library.

Library of Congress Cataloging-in-Publication Data

Balibar, Étienne, 1942-
    Citizenship / Étienne Balibar.
        pages cm
    Includes bibliographical references and index.
    ISBN 978-0-7456-8240-2 (hardback : alk. paper) – ISBN 978-0-7456-8241-9 (pbk. : alk. paper) 1. Citizenship. 2. Citizenship–Philosophy. 3. Democracy. I. Title.
    JF801.B35 2015
    323.6–dc23
                                    2014045196

Typeset in 11 on 14pt Sabon
by Toppan Best-set Premedia Limited
Printed and bound in the UK by CPI Group (UK) Ltd, Croydon, CR0 4YY

For further information on Polity, visit our website: politybooks.com

Contents

Acknowledgments

This essay, written for the collection "I Sampietrini" at the request of my friend Giacomo Marramao, brings together elements that have previously been published separately in both English and French, but have been revised and harmonized. They are, respectively:

- the *Politeia* lecture, which I gave on May 12, 2005 when I received a diploma of Doctor Honoris Causa from the University of Thessaloniki;
- the Cassal Lecture in French Culture "Antinomies of Citizenship," which I gave on May 12, 2009 at the University of London (Institute of Germanic and Romance Studies), published in English in the *Journal of Romance Studies* 10:2, Summer 2010, which was also revised as the introductory essay of my collection *La Proposition de l'égaliberté: Essais politiques et philosophiques 1989–2009* (Paris: PUF, Collection Actuel Marx Confrontations, 2010), now available in English as *Equaliberty: Political Essays*, trans. James Ingram (Durham, NC: Duke University Press, 2013);

- the four lectures "1968–2008: 40 Years Later: Of
  Insurrection and Democracy," given as a "Master
  Class" at the Birkbeck Institute for the Humanities,
  University of London, from May 6 to 15, 2008;
- the lecture "Historical Dilemmas of Democracy and
  Their Contemporary Relevance for Citizenship,"
  given March 17, 2008 for the Colloquium "Citizenship
  in the 21st Century," at the Graduate Program for
  Cultural Studies at the University of Pittsburgh
  (published in English in *Rethinking Marxism* 20:4,
  October 2008).

I wish to thank these universities for their invitations, which
gave me the opportunity to develop various aspects of the
present work.

1

Democracy and Citizenship: An Antinomic Relationship

The concepts of citizenship and democracy are inextricably linked, but this does not mean that the relationship between the two is perfectly reciprocal. A reader who picks up a book with the title *Citizenship* might easily imagine that in the eyes of the author the former trumps the latter, that "democracy" only *qualifies* citizenship, that its relative significance would be a question of secondary importance, to be determined a posteriori. Such questions of hierarchy – or, as Rawls (1971) would say, "lexical priority" – are not peripheral. They are an important battleground in the debate between "republican" (or neo-republican) and "democratic" (liberal or social) views of politics. They constitute the basis of political philosophy's approach, and therefore critiques of it as well, as both Jacques Rancière (1999) and Miguel Abensour (2006) have shown, each in his own way. So it is not simply that I do not wish to subordinate questions of democracy to those of citizenship, I will also maintain that democracy – or, better yet, the "democratic paradox," to borrow Chantal Mouffe's apt expression (2000) – is the determining feature of the problem around which political philosophy orbits, precisely because democracy is what makes the institution of citizenship *problematic*.

Citizenship has taken various forms across history. To be sure, we must be quite careful to avoid conflating these together. But we must also ask what it is that has been transmitted *under this name*, through its successive "translations." Underneath all of them there runs an underlying analogy, which stems from the antinomy between citizenship and democracy as a dynamic for the *transformation of the political*. In using the term "antinomic" to describe this constituent relationship of citizenship – a relationship that also, of course, puts citizenship in crisis – I am drawing on a Western philosophical tradition that has emphasized two ideas in particular: (1) the permanent tension between the positive and the negative, between the processes of construction and destruction; and (2) the persistence of a problem that can be neither "definitively" resolved nor utterly eradicated. My working hypothesis will be that at the heart of the institution of citizenship there is a contradiction with regard to democracy, one that continually emerges and re-emerges. I will endeavor to identify the moments of a *dialectical process*, in which both the movements and conflicts of a complex history would appear, as well as the conditions necessary for joining together theory and practice.

It goes perhaps without saying that the pairing of citizenship with democracy is not a "natural" one. It was entirely historically determined. That being said, I plan to follow an intellectual path that spans from Aristotle to Marx – albeit with some detours – while passing through Spinoza. In Book III of *The Politics* (*Ta Politika*), Aristotle (2009) argues that all political regimes involving citizens who are "office-holders" for either a definite or indefinite term (*aoristos archē*) will always involve an element of democracy that cannot be eliminated in favor of other forms of government. His goal, however, is to mitigate the risks of this by transforming democracy into "timocracy" (as he calls it in the *Nichomachean Ethics*). In our modern era, the direction of this argument has been reversed: first by Spinoza in his unfinished *Tractatus Politicus* (2005 [1677]) – although for him democracy was not so much a specific type of regime as it was the tendency in monarchical or aristocratic regimes for power to devolve into the hands of the multitude; and then by the young Marx, who, in his 1843 *Critique of Hegel's "Philosophy of Right"* (1970 [1843]), explicitly held that democracy – or "legislative authority" – was the "truth of all constitutions." More recently, Rancière has returned to this thesis by showing that no regime can completely eliminate the risk posed by the necessity of gaining acceptance from its people, who can *decide to obey – or not.* Antonio Negri (1999) sees this as the central theme of an "affirmative" theory of the *constituent power* of the "multitude." States that monopolize all of the instruments of power will continually seek to replace this capacity with forms of *constituted power.*

I believe that we must *interpret* this fundamental formulation rather differently than the authors above have, by adopting a dialectical perspective. It is the antinomy lodged at the heart of the relationship between citizenship and democracy that has been, in its successive forms, the motor for the transformation of the political institution. This is why, historically speaking, the label "democratic citizenship" can refer only to a persistent problem, an interplay of conflicts and antithetical definitions, an enigma with no definitive solution – even if periodically, in the context of a decisive *invention*, it has been declared that a solution has "finally been discovered" (Marx) or that a "lost treasure" has been either found or reconquered (Arendt).

Such formulations imply a specific conception of political philosophy, whose assumptions and counterarguments would have to be examined in detail. I prefer not to engage directly with this debate here. Not because it is purely speculative; on the contrary, its implications are quite concrete and

practical. But rather because I hope to show how these
formulations can emerge via the examination of another
hypothesis: namely, there are situations and moments in
which the antinomy of citizenship becomes especially *visible*.
The fact that it is impossible to either reject all forms of citizenship or perpetuate a specific constitution of it indefinitely
will lead to an exhaustion of the very meaning of the word
"politics" itself, whose prevailing usages will then come to
seem either obsolete or perverse.

It seems as if today we find ourselves in just such a situation. This has profound implications for definitions and specific conceptions that had, for a long time, seemed indisputable
(such as those of "national citizenship" or "social citizenship"), but also, beyond that, for the category of *citizenship*
itself, whose transformative power – its historical capacity
to reinvent itself – suddenly seems to have been annihilated.
Against this background I will then examine (starting with
Wendy Brown's interpretation) the "neo-liberal" mode of
governance as a process of the "de-democratization of
democracy" that may or may not be reversible. For my part,
I see it as an expression of the *destructive* character inherent
in the antinomies of citizenship, and thus a challenge that
will face any contemporary attempt to rethink the capacities
of collective politics.

I plan to explore several aspects of this dialectic.

The first, and this still emerges in contemporary debates,
concerns the scope of what the ancient Greeks (particularly
the Athenians, for whom Aristotle would later make himself
the theoretician of institutions) called the "constitution of
citizenship" (*politeia*). This idea preceded the appearance of
the division between "civil society" and "state," which
would irreversibly install the body politic within the space
created by this scission. But it also gave rise to the dual ideas
of power as the "indefinite office" of citizens and of reciprocal obligations as a necessary condition of their autonomy.

The second concerns the *legacy* of the "bourgeois" revolutions undertaken in the name of *equaliberty (égaliberté)* in the history of modern citizenship, understood as national citizenship (or citizenship in the *nation-state*). We can identify this influence as a continuing interplay or differential of insurrection and constitution, which constantly gives rise to the question of how the universal can be realized within the form (and limits) of a *community* that is organized by the state. The contradictions in this process are particularly visible in the confrontation between different theories and different practices of *representation* – given that representation is not simply an "authorization" of *representatives*, but actually a power, or even an "action," of the *represented*.

The third aspect comes from the internal contradictions of "social citizenship" as it has come to be constituted – essentially in Europe – within the framework of the *social-national state (État national-social)* – an expression that, out of concern for precision, I prefer to the terms "Welfare State," *État-Providence*, or *Sozialstaat* employed in various European countries. This means that while historically this form of citizenship represents a democratic achievement, albeit within certain *limits*, of course, this in turn paradoxically functions as an impediment to future progress, despite the fact that the idea of *progress* is inherent in it. It is particularly important to explore these limits (and to expand our understanding of their scope) in two correlative directions: the examination of the relationship between *citizenship and social exclusion* and of the relationship between *citizenship and civil conflict*.

The fourth aspect concerns what has come to be called the "neo-liberal" reaction to the crisis of the social-national state (or, depending on one's view, the role played by neo-liberalism in triggering this crisis), which has consisted in the promotion of individualism and "rational self-interest" above all, along with the privatization of public sector functions and services. To what extent does this pose a truly mortal threat to citizenship – not only to its *past* forms, but also to *those to come*? To what extent can we imagine that neo-liberalism contains, at least in a negative form, the premises of a *new configuration* of citizenship outside of its traditional institutions (namely, *representative democracy*, which neo-liberals tend to try to replace with various forms of "governance" and "mass communication")? Here I will try to demonstrate, *a contrario*, the inescapability of the citizenship/democracy dialectic, by superimposing onto it the opposition between "de-democratization" and the "democratization of democracy" as a *recourse* for citizenship. It is to this last idea that I will dedicate my provisional conclusion.

2

Politeia

The era in which certain European nations or nations born of European expansion saw themselves as the center of the world has come to an end. Various critiques of the Eurocentric perspective have endeavored to show how the problematics of classical political philosophy do not apply to "most of the world" (Chatterjee, 2004). Nevertheless, it must still be possible to endow certain political constructions that have emerged from the Western tradition with a certain universal character. Not universal in the sense of extensive, territorial, and all-encompassing, but rather in the sense of an intensive universality; one that would ideally turn political institutions into instruments for universalizing social relationships, a means of removing the barriers between citizens and of toppling forms of domination that subjugate them – even if, as we have seen, these two perspectives can never be fully independent from one another.

The current situation has rendered these questions all the more pressing and has led them to cluster around certain core terms, which can be difficult to translate from one language to another, even when they have their roots in a shared historical and cultural space. The most obvious example of this is undoubtedly *constitution*. For the past several years there have been periodic moments when a "European constitution" was to be adopted, following procedures that varied from country to country, which was to solemnly mark the continent's transformation into an autonomous ensemble of a novel kind for which there is no real historical precedent. The Italian word *constituzione* (equivalent to "constitution" in French or in English) is *Verfassung* in German and *syntagma* in modern Greek, all of which place the emphasis on the construction of a body politic, the joining together of its various parties and the institutional production of unity and public interest. But there is a good chance that the spirit animating the creation of a European philosophy is now being steered, both by linguistic feeling and by historical debates over the essence of the political and its translation into law, in the direction of a different term, one that comes from ancient Greece: *politeia*. The Romans "translated" this as *res publica*, and the British of the classical period translated it first as *polity*, then as *commonwealth*, adopting alternate ancient etymologies. Out of these terms came the belief, which is still widely held today, in the universality of the political and legal form and in a movement of progressive and persistent expansion, first from city to nation-state, and from there to post-national communities, perhaps even the whole cosmopolitan space. At the same time, one does wonder to what extent this category contains an unchanging kernel of meaning, and whether its application to a context that is now quite removed from its initial articulation might not in truth involve a great deal of illusion and ideological mystification. For these reasons, among others, I shall provide a brief examination of the contemporary relevance of the concept of *politeia*, specifically Aristotle's conception of it, and of the nature or limits of its universality.

For perhaps the first time since Aristotle set about describing the organizational forms of the ancient Greek cities, to which he ascribed norms of internal equilibrium that he saw as both rational and in accordance with nature, it is possible to see the two aspects that overlapped quite closely in the Greek conception of *politeia* as two sides of the same problem, which we could group together in a single concept entitled the "constitution of citizenship." On the one hand there is reciprocity, the distribution and rotation of "power," of "office" (*archē*), among the rights-holders in the city, and, on the other hand, there is the organization of administrative and governmental duties (or "offices") into a system of legal institutions. The *politeia* gave this conjunction effective form, although within certain extremely strict limits and contingent on massive exclusions. But the later developments of the state would tear the two apart, seemingly forever, through the constitution of sovereign territory and the grouping of populations under exclusive and quasi-hereditary ethnic or religious labels. Now, however, this combination of the two could again serve as a working hypothesis, a possibility once more within the context of what is called "globalization" and post-national political constructions.

This *possibility* is obviously not *necessary*, and perhaps not even *probable*, given that it is not the dominant trend at this moment. What we are seeing now is the proliferation and increased fortification of borders, which has also resulted in a change in their status. But this could be the *question* that will return insistently, putting pressure on the contradictions and aporias of the de-territorialization and re-territorialization of relationships of power. This could be the question that implicitly offers a multifaceted alternative to the processes of neutralizing and eventually annihilating the political that stem from the dominance of the capitalist market economy and communications technology. This might correspond to the "beautiful risk" (*kalos kindunos*, to quote Plato, *Phaedra*, 114 d) of a *continuation of the political*, of a renewal or reconstitution beyond the relative exhaustion of its properly modern forms.

As we explore this hypothesis, we must ask ourselves whether we can realistically affirm the paradoxical picture of a constitution of citizenship that is both *open*, transnational, and "cosmopolitan," as well as *evolving*, "expansive," to use a category that Gramsci (1992) applied to democracy, or as always "to come," to borrow a formulation that consistently appeared in Jacques Derrida's later work (2005). This is a *conflictual* picture of a citizenship, one that remains inspired by the *politeia* model, but at the price of upending or inverting most of the anthropological presuppositions upon which it had rested up until now.

The "Constitution of Citizenship" and the "Invention of Democracy"

Let us return to what *politeia* meant in the context of the Greek city states, and attempt to provide an overview of some of its characteristic tensions, specifically through the lens of Aristotle's presentation. It is almost a commonplace among Hellenists, philosophers, and legal historians to explain that the meaning of the Greek word *politeia* not only refers to different content from one author to another, but also "diverges" into two heterogeneous semantics. This is clearly an anachronism. When Aristotle uses the word *politeia* twice, in two distinct contexts, the term must certainly refer to a complex, evolving meaning, but it will not mean two radically different things. This anachronistic reading is revelatory of the gulf that has opened between the establishment of politics within the context of the Greek city, particularly in Athens, to which Aristotle is referring, and the institution of politics within the context of the modern nation-state, including its democratic form, where it is used to identify what distinguishes singularly "political bodies" from other types of groupings or associations.

Here I will cite Francis Wolff, an eminent specialist on Aristotle, in his article "Polis" in *Dictionary of Untranslatables: A Philosophical Lexicon*:

> The *polis* is thus neither a nation, nor a state, nor a society. [...] What constitutes the *polis* is the identity of the sphere of power (which for us concerns the "state") with the sphere of community (which for us is organized into "society"), and it is to this unity that each individual feels affectively bound (and not to the "nation"). [...] This is why the *polis* is neither the state nor society, but the "political community." [...] If the *politês* is defined as a person who participates in this *polis*, the *politeia* may be either the subjective bond of the *politês* to the *polis*, that is, the way in which the *polis* as a community distributes among those whom it recognizes as its participants (the "citizenry"), or the objective organization of the functions of government and administration, that is, the way in which the power of the *polis* is collectively guaranteed (the "form of government" or the "constitution"). (Cassin, 2014: 802)

My colleague refers to the famous tri-partition of political regimes, in which power is either exercised by one, several, or all citizens, that has long dominated political philosophy. He implicitly evokes the fluctuations in the names given to these regimes, names heavily laden with value judgments: *tyranny* or *monarchy*, *aristocracy* or *oligarchy*, *democracy* or *isonomy*. This is what led him to point out the crucial problem in the interpretation of Aristotle's thinking, which is the fact that Aristotle again uses the same word, *politeia*, to refer to constitutional rule "par excellence," which distributes power among all citizens according to the "common good" (*pros to koinon sumpheron*). It would seem then that

Aristotle gives, or at least appears to give, this term a third, either redundant or reflexive, meaning.

There is another possible reading, however. The term *politeia* never has a single meaning, even if we are obliged to render it in English or modern Italian as a composite expression, such as the "constitution of citizenship" – here meaning constitution in the full sense of the word: not just a legal text, but also the historical process of constitution or of societal and institutional social formation. It has always been a question of "educating" or "configuring" the citizen, the carrier of political action, by formulating an explicit list of rights, duties, and powers, and in prescribing the modalities of his – and more recently her – existence. This is as true now as it has ever been. Take, for example, the fact that we are told that federated or confederated Europe will be given a "constitution," notwithstanding the more or less unsatisfactory forms this idea has taken up to this point. In the final analysis, the validity, the coherency, the temporal solidity of such a project will be judged by the manner in which it will define new rights, new duties, new powers; whether it succeeds or fails to give rise to a historically new kind of "citizen." To say that it is not clear this will happen is putting it lightly, if only because of the fragility of the geopolitical framework inside of which this attempt is being made, the strength of the interests opposed to it, and the violence of the social tensions that have arisen within the context of economic globalization. But it is also clear that if it were to succeed, some part of the power, the intrinsic energy, of the old concept would be reactivated, albeit with a different content and in an altogether different context.

But let us return once again to the way Aristotle presented the meaning of the Ancient *politeia*, particularly in Book III of *The Politics*. He defines this concept in three moments, in what is either a dialectical progression or a quite remarkable approximation of it. Here are the three characteristics described in this definition in three stages:

- First (this is the most general definition, the most abstract one, an example of which is given on 1275 a30), a *politeia* exists, which is to say that there are "citizens" and as a result a "city law," where the individuals who constitute it and rotate between different positions of power exercise an *aoristos archē*: an indefinite office, temporally indefinite, but also indefinite with respect to its object and its modalities, which makes them the "sovereigns," or "masters," of the community to which they themselves belong (*kurioi* or *kuriôtatoi*).

- Second (this is the principal, discriminating, definition, given on 1277 a25), there exists a *politeia* between those who, depending on the circumstances, can alternately be in the position of giving orders (*archein*) or receiving them (*archesthai*), who are at one moment ordering and another obeying, and in this sense rotate freely among positions of power.

- Thirdly and finally (this is the final definition given on 1282 a25 and following passages and repeated in Book V, on 1301 a25), a *politeia* exists where the powers or "offices" (still *archai*) are "proportionally" (*isos*) distributed among the citizens relative to their competencies or capabilities and in accordance with the law (*nomos*). In this Aristotle expresses his belief, or his hope, in the city as a concrete, stable form, which is what would allow it to effectively attain its natural goal, which is the common good or the possibility of a "good life" for its members.

Each moment in this progression, which is obviously guided by a political "preference" that for Aristotle had to be founded in both reason and nature – which we might call his ideological *pre-commitment* – gives rise to its own fundamental questions. Let us examine them systematically, before passing on to the investigation of why it is that this synthetic formulation of the problem of citizenship was, in a certain sense, "lost" once it was removed from the context of the city, all while continuing to haunt the political space as an ideal or as something repressed.

The idea of indefinite office (*aoristos archē*) is clearly linked to one of Aristotle's most radical arguments. Aristotle saw this argument as part of the series of reforms designated in classical Athens by the category of *isonomia*, and it brings him closer to certain Sophists while opposing him directly to Plato. According to this argument, the essence, the foundation, of any *political* regime lies in the sovereignty of its own citizens. According to Aristotle, it would be contradictory for power not to belong, in the last resort, to those for whose benefit it was established. This thesis has never ceased to be problematic. It has been systematically attacked by the many diverse authoritarian political traditions, which all make a variant on the same argument that the multitude of citizens are incapable of governing themselves. On the other hand, it was also periodically reaffirmed: by Machiavelli, by Rousseau, by the young Marx, by Tocqueville, and more recently by Arendt, and in the end it came to appear inseparable from the very idea of political universalism. Is it a utopian ideal, or perhaps only purely formal or symbolic? This may very well be the case, but Aristotle gave it quite precise content, arguing that for the multitude of citizens it corresponded to their *effective participation* in the two great responsibilities, which were, on the one hand, *boulein*, deliberation and decision within the framework of popular assemblies, and, on the other, *krinein*, the exercise of legal duties. It also raises a question that is not, strictly speaking, that of the division of powers, but rather of whether there are certain "protected" areas of political life that would be *in their very nature* beyond the competencies of the citizenry. Then there is also the question of whether popular sovereignty can ever become purely "representative," completely transformed into a legal fiction, or whether it must always involve a certain degree of true participation, of "active" citizenship or self-governance. It also opens the question, without giving any definitive answer, of how the real and the virtual are distributed in the idea of democratic sovereignty.

The idea of alternating between governed and governing – to *dunasthai archein te kai archestai* (1277 a25) – and the corresponding moral idea according to which it is by obeying that we learn to command and it is by exercising the responsibilities of authority that we learn to obey (1277 b8–10) – which is what properly speaking constitutes the virtue (*arete*) of a citizen – places the mechanisms of *reciprocity* at the heart of citizenship. It therefore already represents a strong argument in favor of what we would later, in more Roman language, call *equal liberty*, not only as *status* but also in *practice*. Aristotle offers a positive take on the negative, polemical, statement that Herodotus (who had been a student of the Sophists) placed in the mouth of Persian Prince Otanes: without an equal distribution of power, I wish to neither command nor obey (*oute archein oute archesthai ethelô*). In other words: either democracy or anarchy! But this conception of equal liberty as a reciprocity of powers and obligations is immediately accompanied by a radical *limitation* of citizenship. Reciprocity can only exist, for Aristotle and his contemporaries, between those who are equal *by nature*. This means that at the core of the political there is a mechanism for discrimination on the basis of anthropological difference: gender difference, age difference, the difference between manual and intellectual capacities, specifically insofar as it justifies the institution of slavery. (Aristotle was well aware that in Athens a large section of the citizenry were peasants or artisans, but he retained the aristocratic view, which Plato had taken to its extreme, that held that there was something "servile" about manual labor as such.)

This opens up not just a gap, but an abyss. The principle that establishes the intensive, or qualitative, universality of *demos* also involves a seemingly insurmountable quantitative exclusion. And we know that, far from relieving this tension, modern universalism's transformation of the equal liberty of citizens into the *rights of man and citizen* within the national framework has in fact aggravated it. This tension did not prevent the emergence of social movements and struggles that led to entire categories that had previously been excluded, such as women or laborers, becoming or re-becoming citizens; what it did entail, however, was that those who have been excluded from citizenship (and there are always old or new categories that are) are represented, and so to speak "produced," by all sorts of disciplinary or institutional mechanisms, as imperfect human beings, as "abnormals" or monsters on the margins of humanity.

We have not yet escaped, and are perhaps not even close to escaping, from this contradiction. It would require not just a political revolution, but also an ethical and philosophical one – which we are far from achieving, even if its principles are clearly formulated in works like Arendt's (1951) – to arrive at a universal "right to rights," or, better yet, at the idea that the *politeia* does not solely consist in establishing reciprocity on the basis of a *given*, pre-existing – or at least allegedly pre-existing – equality, but in *widening the scope* of the sphere of equality, actively *producing* it as a "fiction," constantly transgressing the limits imposed by "nature" (or that which goes by this name, which is actually tradition). It is probably not happenstance that the "dialectical reversal" of the traditional philosophical formulation of the "rights of man and citizen" came from a woman, who was also an avid reader of the Greeks and was familiar with their distinction between *nomos* and *phusis*.

Finally, as to the conception of the law (*nomos*) as the proportional "distribution" of offices and civic responsibilities, there arises an analogous tension, one which cannot perhaps be separated in practice from the tension between reciprocity and exclusion, but which we should also be careful not to conflate with it simplistically. It seems here as if Aristotle retracts what he had originally conceded in the name of *aoristos archē*. It appears as if he wishes to limit the effects of the sovereignty of the *demos* in the name of the rational exigencies of the common good and good government. To use Rancière's striking terminology: it is not only that all citizens, who are nominally sovereign, do not have an equal share in the established power structure, and notably in the power to make decisions, but that from this point of view there must also necessarily be those who are "share-less" – individuals and categories whose share is denied, and for whom chances to obey will always outnumber chances to take charge or take initiative, who are expected to be passive more often than active. This seems to be the price exacted by the establishment of *consensus*, of *equilibrium* or *homonoia*, of political stability. Or rather, it is the price to be paid for the replacement of conflict (the class struggle in the general sense, but also the struggle between "majorities" and "minorities" or all kinds) with consensus, and therefore *the relegation of these conflicts to outside the public space*; with the exception that – and we have learned how to recognize this – the repressed conflict will always re-emerge, will always return anew, if indeed on new battlefields, in a manner that can be either productive or destructive. It might be that within certain limits and in certain forms, the acceptance and recognition of conflict in the public sphere constitute a *necessary condition* for institutional equilibrium itself, or, at the very least, for "dynamic" equilibrium. This was Machiavelli's theory, which today seems increasingly relevant, at both the national or continental level, but especially at the *global* level. However, here again, we must note that the tension inherent in the concept of the *politeia*, which we could call its "differential" of activity and passivity, or of democracy and oligarchy, has in no way been resolved by the advent of modern constitutions, but indeed has been ratcheted up to a higher level.

Everything comes down to the way in which the people's sovereignty is positively established. Modern constitutionalism has made it a principle for *legitimating* representative mechanisms for delegating power. But it has also had a tendency to subordinate the exercise of popular sovereignty, citing the risk of anarchy and its perversion into totalitarianism, to certain meta-legal "basic norms," which are derived from the principle of the balance of powers or guarantees of individual rights, which are clearly necessary, but are apparently acquired once and for all. It should be said, however, that there is another possible way to conceive of the question of the rules and guarantees to which popular sovereignty must subject itself as a sort of *self-limitation* of its own power, which is the basis of its rationality (as opposed to a theological or mystical conception of sovereignty). This alternative is what Claude Lefort (1981), to use one example, calls the *continued invention* of democracy. It is not that we must throw out constitutions in favor of insurrections, but rather that we must place the insurrectional power to emancipate at the core of political constitutions. We should think of the "Charters of Fundamental Rights" (with, first and foremost, the Universal Declaration of the Rights of Man) as symbolic expressions of the ensemble of powers that the "people" have acquired over the course of their history, the sum of their emancipatory movements, serving as footholds for future inventions, rather than buttressing the established order and limiting future struggles for freedom and equality a priori.

Autonomy or Autarchy of the Political

Before moving on, it would be useful to address an episte-mological consideration. The above propositions do not simply represent a mode of constituting citizenship within the universal modality and – dialectically – the mark of quite profound tensions inherent in universality itself. They also express the idea of the *autonomy of the political*. But they express it in the form, and under the condition, of the *autarchy of the polis*, of the "community of citizens." This, in turn, has two symmetrical traits, which a certain critical tradition, notably Marxist, has had a tendency to perceive as simply two sides of an *idealization of the political*. It is not necessarily clear, however, that they are in fact march-ing in lock-step. How far can we successfully draw the two apart?

On the one hand, making the political autonomous places it on a "plane of immanence," corresponding to either a radical de-theologization or a critique of any transcendent foundation. The *politeia* is a system of *relationships* that citizens establish among *themselves*, because it emerges out of the development of their own conflicts of interests and values. This relationship is not subjugated to any transcend-ent authority, whether it be the Idea of the Good (Plato), or the idea of humanity hypostasizing into a "Great Being" (Comte) or a "community of ends" (Kant). There is therefore no unifying principle that could be imposed on everyone and that would belong to no one. More precisely, the only over-arching principle is *the community itself*, as a totality, a *polis* to which citizens "belong" because they have established it.

Here we encounter the symmetrical aspect of this: *autar-chy* should be understood as, at the very least, relative isola-tion with regard to the outside world, the *cosmos*, and to the *oikoumēnē* ("inhabited world") where historical com-munities dispersed and became individualized. But it should also be understood as an *independence* or a "cultural" liberation with respect to the *material conditions* of life, of human production and reproduction, with the potential result that these, along with all of their corresponding practices (work, sexuality and maternity, the education of children), might be relegated to a domestic sphere of *internal exclusion*, which, as we noted above, has historically corresponded to the institution of patriarchy and slavery.

We should note that, at the philosophical level, the construction of the autonomy of the political within the constricting form of autarchy corresponds perfectly to the division between *nomos* and *phusis* that was at the core of ancient Greek thought and around which these different tendencies position themselves, as around a point of heresy. Public life comes from the *nomos* or the institution, while domestic activities are a *natural* condition. We can also observe that with the phenomenon of "globalization," the two meanings of autarchy have been, in a certain sense, fused together. To discuss the material conditions for the existence of a *politeia*, whether they are drawn from the economy of labor and trade or the bio-economy and bio-politics of populations and the survival of the human race, is *ipso facto* to discuss the relationship that each "community of citizens" maintains with the ensemble of other human societies (including the most "primitive") and that thereafter determine it from within – whether it be a question of class composition and social conflicts, or of modes of communication and cultural development. In other words, by becoming *fused together* over time, the "autarchic" limitations of the *politeia* have irreparably collapsed as "borders." It is no longer possible for any society, any *polis* in the metaphorical sense of the word, to construct itself (if indeed this had ever been possible) within such limits, except in an imaginary sense. It can only exist now as an *open city*, opening onto different "externalities" that condition it from *within*, which may seem to be a contradiction in terms. Or, in other words, the idea of the autonomy of the political – as an autonomization of *collective action*, and as a radically secular relationship to the self, immanent in the "body politic" (the system of social relationships and the dynamic of internal conflicts) – can only have meaning today if we renounce once and for all the myth of autarchy and the others that accompany it (from autochthony to the untranslatable specificity of every culture). Although we have neither guarantee nor certainty, we must make this leap into the project of building a community of citizens that would be *open* in principle, but that would not as a result forfeit the ideas of rights and obligations or of the distribution of powers and collective participation in *self-government*. As we have observed in the debates surrounding environmentalism and "globalism," there has also been a profound transformation, although evidently an *unfinished* one, in the opposition between nature and the institution (or the *phusis* and the *nomos*), which certain political philosophers have seen as a new materialism, while others, on the contrary, have viewed it as an argument in favor of a generalized artificialism.

Politeia and the "Withering Away of the State"

Let us return to my initial aim. Once again, it is a question not of providing solutions or of giving answers, but rather of formulating a question that will serve as a guiding thread for what is to come. Would we be justified in assuming that a renewed examination of the dominant form of nation-state citizenship will, paradoxically, *reopen* the dialectics inherent in the concept of *politeia*? That it will revive, in other words, the question of how to hold together the demands of the reciprocal recognition of rights – which I am tempted to call the "pressure of equal liberty" – and the demands of the regulation of social conflicts, of the *self-limitation* of the exercise of power. Nothing seems further removed from our contemporary European perspectives, and yet two types of argument can be brought to bear, one negative, one positive.

On the negative side, we can observe that we have undergone a very long historical cycle through imperial, urban, and finally state forms of government, during which the principle of citizenship was alternately lost and reconstituted by identifying itself with the construction of nations – as can be seen in the use of such terms as the Anglo-American *citizenship* or the modern German *Staatsbürgerschaft*. In its urban medieval and renaissance form, the principle of ancient-style citizenship survived as a historical exception. (See Marx Weber's [1957 (1921)] analysis of the city [*Stadt*], which he defined as a form of "illegitimate domination," which is to say, an institution of power with no transcendental "guarantee," eternally exposed to the risk of insurrection.) But this cycle, in all its complexity, nonetheless fundamentally contributed to the translation of citizenship into the language of the *state*, or its subordination to the functioning of the state. The "people" therefore incrementally became a function of the state. They became incorporated, perhaps even *assimilated*, into the state. "*Ich, der Staat, bin das Volk*" ("I, the state, am the people"), to quote Nietzsche's terribly ironic phrase from the beginning of *Thus Spoke Zarathustra* (1978 [1885]: 75), written at the very moment when the imperial European powers were "dividing up the world" at the Congress of Berlin. Modern constitutions (which have been attacked on this very point by Negri [1999]) have adopted the habit of defining "constituent power" not as an insurrectional power, but as *a state function*, for example as the right to revise the constitution within the forms and limits that it sets out for itself, or to periodically replace those in power.

Naturally, this evolution presupposes a deep collective feeling that identifies individuals and intermediary social bodies with the higher-level state community. The consequences of this extend beyond pathology or repression. It represents, undeniably, *alienation* in the philosophical sense of the term, even in the "freest" states. This alienation, with its dual features of protection and constraint, has reached its peak in the most evolved form of the European nation-state as a *community of passive citizens*: the social democratic state, or, as we will call it later, the "social-national" state. We know that such states – where and to the extent that they have existed – were the results of an age-old confrontation with social and political movements that represented forms of *active citizenship*, and even certain forms of insurrectional demand-making. Actively demanding citizenship brought the permanence of conflict into the core of the sphere of the formalized state. This is what could lead us to say that, in the extreme, in the state configuration of the political there is no "democracy" in the pure or ideal sense of the term, but that there could always be a process of *democratization* – which is in truth perhaps more important.

But up to what point, up to what moment? And therefore, within what limits does democratization occur? It is quite difficult to say. At the very least it seems clear that the answer depends on the capacity for survival of the system by which collective identification with the state, the development of bureaucracy as the intermediary between citizens and their own practices, are joined with the practices and movements of the organized social struggle, more often than not within a national framework. The results of this have necessarily been ambiguous. From this point of view it is extremely revealing that the institutions of the revolutionary labor movement have always started in internationalism only to end up in nationalism. Even the movements of solidarity with anti-colonial emancipatory struggles did not, in the end, lead to any lasting changes. But today this mindset has perhaps reached its limits. In any event it has suddenly shown an extreme internal weakness, poorly camouflaged by the proliferation of bureaucracies and "supra-national" legal bodies. We saw this when the European Union asked its nominally sovereign (although at the second degree) "citizens" to perform their state-given "constituent" role – even though the EU itself is nothing more than the ghost of a state, as it includes no truly effective element of collective identification. On the other hand, there is the fact that despite the economic crisis, it wishes to avoid confrontation with any general social movement that would be capable of transnationalizing political conflict. Perhaps such a structure offers a prefiguration of the form in which the state institution of citizenship will *survive* in the years to come, and it might, in fact, represent a form of *statism without a state*, under the name of *governance*. For this reason, there is a high chance that the weakening of the national form of state citizenship will lead only to emptiness, or an anti-political reaction, in the form of resurgent populism or nationalism, for example.

In other words, what we are seeing is a *vacillation* of the age-old balance between the *politeia* and the state (or the *imperium*). On its own, this vacillation has not yet sparked a renewal of the democratic dynamic. It has certainly not resulted in a pure and simple *return* to the communal and autarchic pre-state forms. Instead, it has led to a period of extreme danger for the democratic tradition, a phase that could last for quite a long time. But let us again remember that even if the crisis does not make a renewal *necessary*, and is perhaps not even particularly favorable to it, it does not present a *fatal* obstacle to it either. In a certain sense it makes its urgency all the more apparent. It is therefore a *negative* precondition for a return to the problem of the *politeia*.

"Civil Society": The New Location of the *Politeia?*

What, then, would the positive condition be? Here we must operate at an even more hypothetical – if not speculative – level. We must ask ourselves what forms could possibly be taken by, or might currently be taken by, "constituent processes" – or *elements of post-state citizenship*, which are necessarily *disjointed*, even fragmented and relegated to the extremities of the political space, but which are nonetheless "destined" to find each other, or which could be brought together through our efforts. Where could such elements be found? Where even do we begin to look for them?

One answer to this question, which has been in vogue for quite some time, is *civil society*. This has actually been a point upon which Marxists and post-Marxists, theoreticians of "anti-systemic movements" and liberal thinkers, have been able to agree – at least verbally. It cannot be denied that civil society made many of the emblematic political phenomena of our era possible, particularly new dimensions of active citizenship that are not reducible to the formalism of the state or the national framework (Cohen and Arato, 1992). For this reason, it is very important to emphasize the way in which the state has essentially *lagged behind*, remaining stuck within the framework of the nation, or simply attempted to transpose this form onto a higher level. Civil society, on the other hand, is seen as extending out transnationally, across borders – a "commercial" society, in the full classical sense of the term, despite the obstacles raised by the heterogeneity of languages and cultures (or using these as an opportunity to create new forms of communication).

It might seem as if the category of the "multitude," as Hardt and Negri (2000, 2004, 2009) employ it, is simply a radicalization (and also an idealization) of this answer, as its symmetry with the concept of the *imperium* would suggest.

The problem with such a simple reading is the fact that embedded in their conception of the multitude is a *division* between its constituent force and the social forms imposed by capitalist development. It is therefore a decomposition rather than an autonomization of "civil society." Then there is the fact that, for Hardt and Negri, the "empire" that the multitude opposes ("resists") is not a purely "private" or "corporate" structure, but includes the state as well, even if, in line with the Marxist tradition – to which Hardt and Negri are, at least on this point, entirely faithful – to them the state is nothing more than a *function* of the capitalist system. State and civil society are not external to each other. And, finally, there is the fact that Hardt and Negri look for a principle of resistance and a power specific to the multitude *underneath* the relationships and institutions that constitute civil society, in the "ontology of productive forces," which are vitalist in nature or, when they borrow Foucault's terminology, "biopolitical." Hardt and Negri's powerful and provocative argument therefore contributes to the problematization of the idea of "civil society" as the new location of the political, rather than offering it up as an answer.

There are several weaknesses with identifying the *politeia* to come with the power of "civil society" as a new "political society," although both contemporary context and ancient ideas seem to be pushing in that direction. The first is that the category of "civil society" includes certain forces, institutions, and tendencies that are not only not *democratic* in any way, but aren't even *political* in the sense of the term that we are trying to recover by tracing back to its origins. These are, first and foremost, the forces and structures of capitalist markets, which have swallowed up the production and commercialization not only of material goods, but also of life (or of *care*) and culture. These forces that dominate "civil society" constitute the *matter*, but also represent the antitheses and obstacles to the "civic" movements to come. It is not a question of destroying these forces so much as it is of mastering them, and therefore thwarting them, in such a way as to channel economic power into the service of the common good of society, and, beyond that, of the many societies that make up humanity. What we should inscribe *positively*, among the factors in the reconstitution of the *politeia* beyond the state, or rather beyond the monopoly of the state and the crisis of the state, is not civil society as such, but the *differences between tendencies* within civil society, specifically the confrontation between the logics of public interest and private interest that takes place within it.

There is another drawback to this reference to civil society, seen either as a certain kind of fetish or as a shibboleth, that we can attempt to turn into an advantage or a positive recommendation. This is that it excludes, or seems to exclude, the institutional forms and organization that are not infra-state or "private," but, on the contrary, supra-state. I am referring not to "alliances," "federations," and "confederations" of states, but to the *global* judicial, economic, environmental, or health organizations that are charged with protecting the collective security and the fight against unequal development, ranging from the United Nations to the World Health Organization to the International Criminal Courts, and passing through the World Bank and the International Monetary Fund. Naturally, in order for there to be the possibility of locating the constitution of citizenship within these institutions – which, at least virtually, are an embodiment of a certain kind of "community without a community," bodies regulating conflicts of interests in the world, founded not on belonging and autarchy, but on universalized reciprocity – would require a radical democratization that still remains very distant. This is because it would require not just the dissolution of their ties to states, which, for the most part, they rely on today, but rather a decisive step "beyond the Leviathan" (Marramao, 1995), towards a sharing and relativization of state sovereignty. It is all too clear the extent to which powerful forces will stubbornly, even violently, resist an inversion of the corridor of transmission between the state *imperium* and the international or global *auctoritas*. This inversion would involve these international organizations acquiring a cosmopolitan authority independent of that of the states. This authority would be rooted in the practices, procedures of intervention, modalities of cooperation, participation, delegation of power, and representation that *bypass* the state level, and *descend* down to the level of the communities of citizens themselves, in order to receive some of these groups' momentum, as they simultaneously establish their legality *at the top*. In the present moment, we can *ask* this question, but we cannot *answer it*. But history does not ask (itself) only questions that it can answer…Or maybe it can only answer them by posing them differently.

3

Aequa Libertas

Having attempted, in my first theoretical approach, to address contemporary questions by pushing the idea of the *politeia* as a "constitution of citizenship" to its very limits, we can now turn our focus to a second genealogy of the antinomies of democratic citizenship: what I have called the *legacy of equaliberty*, using this as an umbrella term to encompass the civic ideals of the "bourgeois" revolutions that occurred over the course of the modern era. Let us not forget that "bourgeois" and "citizen" were originally etymologically synonymous (a *burgher* is a citizen of a free city). The distinction between the two that was emphasized by Rousseau (1968 [1762]) and then by Hegel (1991 [1820]) never fully or completely erased this initial conjunction.

Marx, who took Rousseau and Hegel's scission between "bourgeois" and "citizen" to its breaking point, often said that political modernity appears on the stage of history "dressed in ancient garb," or more specifically, in *Roman garb* (Marx, 2005 [1852]). This should remind us that *aequa libertas* and *aequum ius* are Roman ideas that Cicero, in particular, employed to refer to the essence of the regime that he called *res publica*:

et talis est quaeque respublica, qualis ejus aut natura, aut voluntas, qui illam regit. Itaque nulla alia in civitate, nisi in qua populi potestas summa est, ullum domicilium libertas habet: qua quidem certe nihil potest esse dulcius; et quae, si aequa non est, ne libertas quidemn est. Qui autem aequa potest esse? (Republic, I, 31)

And each commonwealth corresponds to the nature and will of him who governs it. Therefore, in no other constitution than that in which the people exercise sovereign power has liberty any sure abode, than which there certainly is no more desirable blessing. And if it be not equally established for every one, it is not even liberty at all. And how can there be this character of equality, I do not say under a monarchy, where slavery is least disguised or doubtful, but even in those conditions in which the people are free indeed in words, for they give their suffrages, they elect officers, they are canvassed and solicited for magistracies; but yet they only grant those things which they are obliged to grant whether they will or not, and which are not really in their free power, though others ask them for them? (Cicero, 2008: 18–19)

Moreover, while Cicero's political thought did fall within a legal tradition that was specific to Roman institutions, it also emerged from a theorization of *humanitas* that came from Stoic cosmopolitanism, which, via its reformulation by Christianity, appears in the modern era in the form of philosophies of *natural rights*.

What is crucial about its use, however, was the "revolutionary" moment that inaugurated modern politics, in which "equal rights" became a new kind of *universal* (Gauthier, 1998). At that time it was constructed as essentially two pairings of opposites. The first is the unity of *man* and *citizen*, which appear to be coextensive concepts despite all of the practical restrictions regarding the distribution of rights and powers. The second is the unity (or reciprocity) of the concepts of *liberty* and *equality*, which are seen as two sides of the same "constituent power," despite the permanent tendency of bourgeois political ideologies (which we can generally group under the term "liberalism") to confer epistemic, even ontological, priority onto the first term, making it the quintessential "natural right," to which the socialist tendency to privilege equality is a response. This first tendency can be illustrated by what John Rawls (1971) called the "lexical priority" inherent in the principle of equal liberty, the second by Rancière's (2006) idea that there is a radical opposition between democracy as an affirmation of "the power of anybody" and the educational and representative institutions that are so many attempts to limit this principle.

Insurrection and Constitution

What is particularly interesting is the element of tension that stems from these two pairings of opposites; it helps us understand why demands that accrued powers be extended to the people or for emancipation from domination, which translates into new rights, will always take an insurrectional form. By simultaneously demanding equality and liberty, we reiterate the enunciation that is at the root of modern universal citizenship. Undoubtedly, it is in cases when political power is conquered in a manner that is itself revolutionary, involving either regime change (the traditional passage from monarchy to republic, for example) or a dominant class being forced to renounce its privileges, that this enunciation is reiterated in the highest symbolic manner. But the *petitio juris*, the emancipatory movement tied to demands for rights, can manifest itself in an infinite number of ways: through popular movements, democratic campaigns, or the formation of either enduring or short-lived political parties. It involves a power struggle that can be violent or non-violent, depending on the context, as well as the use or rejection of legal forms and existing political institutions. We need only think of the diversity of national histories in Europe when it comes to the conquest of civil, political, or social rights, or of the multiplicity of forms of decolonization in the twentieth century, or of the progression of African-American rights through civil war and civil rights movements over more than a century in the United States, and so on.

While the phenomenology varies, it is also clear that in the end conflict is always the determining factor, because a spontaneous inclination to equaliberty is not inscribed in human nature, and those in power never give up their privileges voluntarily, even if at certain moments they can be caught up in the jubilant camaraderie of the moment – as was the case with the symbolic example of the "Night of August 4, 1789," although one wonders whether events actually transpired in the way that they have been mythologized by republican imagery. Struggles will therefore always be necessary and, even beyond that, a *legitimation of struggle* must be affirmed, what Rancière called *the share of the share-less (part des sans-part)*, that would bestow a universal significance onto the demands of those who have been excluded from the "common good" or the "general will." What we see emerging here is the *essential incompleteness* of "the people" as a body politic, a process of universalization that passes through conflict, and through the "negation" of exclusions from dignity, property, security, and "fundamental rights" in general. Characterized in this way, the insurrectional moment looks both to the future and to the past. To the past, because it draws on the democratic foundation of any constitution whose legitimacy is not derived from tradition, revelation, or simple bureaucratic efficiency, despite how determinative these forms of legitimation might be in the construction of states; and to the future because, in the face of the limitations and exclusions that have shaped the realization of democracy in historical constitutions, the *return to insurrection* (and the return *of insurrection*, which had up until then been held off) represents a permanent possibility. Whether this possibility becomes concrete or not is, of course, a different matter, one that cannot be deduced a priori.

However, if the *political community* rests on the conjunction of citizenship with different insurrectional modalities of emancipation or the conquest of universal rights, it will inevitably take on a paradoxical form. Exclusive of all *consensus*, it cannot be realized as a homogeneous unity of its members, nor can it be represented as a complete totality. This does not mean that it can dissolve into the individualistic picture of an aggregate of economic and social subjects whose only ties would be the "invisible hand" of self-interest, or interdependent needs, or the inverse picture of the "war of all against all," which is to say a generalized antagonism of interests that, *as such*, would be "common." In one sense, therefore, the "citizens" (or fellow citizens) of equaliberty are *neither friends nor enemies*. Their relationships are agonistic in kind. Here we are approaching what Chantal Mouffe (2000) suggested we call the "democratic paradox," an idea to which I will return. We are also at the threshold of the forms through which an institution of citizenship that remains essentially antinomic can manifest itself in history, as names, spaces, and territories change, as do the historical narratives and ideological formations associated with its recognition by subjects who see in it their political horizon and the condition of their existence.

Citizenship and Nationality

Why is the fundamentally unstable, problematic, "contingent" character of democracy not more apparent (or why does it not manifest itself more often)? Why is it that once it manifests itself it is readily designated as a *collapse* of citizenship? This is undoubtedly due to the fact that in the modern era, notions of *citizenship* and *nationality* have become identified together in practice, in what could be considered to be the *founding equation* of the modern "republican" state, which is all the more inarguable and – apparently – indestructible given that the state never stops reinforcing itself, and that its mythical, imaginary, and cultural forms continue to proliferate.

Couldn't we imagine, however, that the historical cycle of the *sovereign nation-state* is coming to an end, as seems to be possible today, in such a way as to make the *contingent* character of this equation visible (once again)? What we are dealing with is an equation that was historically determined, in relation to certain geographical and temporal conditions, that is now being exposed to the erosion and changes of time. It is certainly the case that the absolute sovereignty of the nation-state, as an economic and military power, and even as a capacity to control the movement and communication of its own citizens, has been forcefully put into question during the contemporary period. However, it is not at all clear that this process of trans-nationalization has meant the same thing everywhere, or that the European perception of it could be generalizable. It is quite possible that China's perspective would be quite different, both "semantically" and "historically," owing to the fact that it is currently trying to build itself into a new "hegemonic nation" at the regional and global level. Either way, we are at a moment when it is becoming visible (once again) that national interest and national identity are not *as such, in the absolute*, factors that unify a community of citizens, and also that the equation of *citizenship* with *nationality* is essentially precarious.

However, our analysis cannot end here. No matter how effective the national form has been in the modern period, it is only one of the possible historical forms that a community of citizens can take, and it will never be able to absorb all of the functions of such a community and will never neutralize all of its contradictions. Above all, it is important to understand that while citizenship in general, as a political "idea," certainly involves a reference to a community (just like the idea of citizenship *without institutions*, the idea of citizenship *without community* is almost a contradiction in terms), its essence cannot be located in the *consensus* of its members. Hence the strategic role played by terms such as *res publica* or *commonwealth*, but also their profound ambiguity. *Citizens* as such are always *fellow citizens* (or *co-citizens*, mutually conferring upon each other the rights that they exercise); this reciprocal dimension is constituent. In a famous article, Émile Benveniste (1974) showed that in the last century, from the philological point of view, the priority of reciprocity over belonging could be expressed better by the Latin pairing *civis–civitas* than the Greek *polis–politês*, because the semantic "root" is, on the one hand, the status of the individual in relation to others (the "fellow citizen") and, on the other, the nominal precedence of the whole over its members. This divergence has had significant political and symbolic consequences, which can also be read in the modern legacies of these two discourses. But above all we should understand it as an internal tension, present everywhere, that gives rise to a permanent oscillation.

How, then, could citizens exist outside of a "community," whether territorial or not, whether imagined as a fact of nature or a cultural heritage, defined as a product of history or a purposeful construction? Aristotle, as we already saw, proposed just such a fundamental justification, and in doing so inaugurated political philosophy. For him, the ties between citizens come from a rule of reciprocity between rights and duties. Or to put it better: it rests on the fact that a reciprocal relationship between rights and duties implies both a *limitation on the power of the governing* and *the acceptance of the law on the part of the governed*. In Aristotle's view, what guarantees this reciprocity is the *periodic cycling of positions* between the "governing" (*archôn*) and the "governed" (*archomenons*), but he also saw this principle as running the risk of "ultra-democracy." As a result, the subsequent political tradition never ceased seeking to elaborate the idea of a "mixed constitution" in which reciprocity and hierarchy would be "reconciled" or "combined." Officeholders are therefore responsible before their constituents, and ordinary citizens obey the law that they themselves contributed to instituting, either directly or through the intermediary of representatives.

However, locating citizenship within the horizon of the community is in no way synonymous with consensus or homogeneity. Quite the opposite, in fact, because the rights that it guarantees were *conquered*, which is to say that they were established in the face of resistance from privilege-holders, "particular interests" and authorities representing social "domination." This is because, as Lefort (1981) argues, they were *invented* (and must be once again) – and in this he goes against the dominant trends in both liberalism and republicanism – and their contents, just like those of their corresponding "rights" and "responsibilities," are defined by this conflictual relationship.

Politics and Anti-Politics:
The Dilemma of the Institution

We have now arrived at an essential feature of modern citizenship, one that is also one of the reasons why its history can only be presented as a constant dialectical movement. It is obviously very difficult to square the idea of a *community that has been neither dissolved nor reassembled* with a purely legal or constitutional definition. But it is not impossible to conceive of it as a historical process governed by a law of reproduction, interruption, and permanent transformation. This is the only way to make sense of the discontinuous temporality of the history of citizenship as political institution. Not only has it been riddled with periodic crises and tensions, but it is intrinsically "fragile" or "vulnerable." This is why, over the course of its history, it has been dissolved and reconstituted many times, each time within a new institutional framework. As a constitution of citizenship, it is threatened and destabilized, perhaps even delegitimated (as Weber pointed out), by the very power that makes up its constituent function (or of which it is the "constituted" form): the "insurrectional" power of universalist political movements that aim to conquer rights that do not yet exist, or to widen the scope of existing rights, in such a way as to bring about a situation of equaliberty. This is why it is necessary to speak in terms of a *differential* of insurrection and constitution, which no purely formal or legal representation of the political could adequately summarize.

If this were not the case, we would have to think that democratic inventions, conquests of rights, redefinitions of reciprocities between rights and duties according to larger and more concrete conceptions, stem from some eternal "idea" of citizenship that has always already existed. We would therefore have to replace the idea of *inventing* democracy with the idea of *preserving* it. But a democracy whose role is to "preserve" a certain definition of citizenship is also, there is no doubt, for this very reason incapable of resisting its own "de-democratization." To the extent that politics deals with the transformation of existing realities, their adaptations to changing environments, and the formulation of *alternatives* within an ongoing historical and sociological evolution, such a concept would not be *political* but *anti-political*.

It is therefore important to show how, contrary to any "prescriptive" or "deductive" definition of the political, citizenship has never stopped oscillating between destruction and reconstruction on the basis of its *own* historical institutions. The insurrectional moment associated with the principle of equaliberty is not simply foundational, it is also the enemy of institutional stability. And if we admit that in its realizations, of varying levels of completeness, it represents the universal at the heart of the political field, we will also have to admit that history contains no *appropriations* or *installations* in the "realm" of the universal, in the way that classical political philosophers thought that the arrival of the Rights of Man and Citizen would represent a point of no return, a moment when mankind at long last became in reality the bearer of the universal that had always been its destiny.

If we combine this idea of a differential of insurrection and constitution with the representation of a community without unity, always undergoing reproduction and transformation, the dialectic that we end up with does not remain purely speculative. The conflicts that it entails can sometimes be quite violent. And they affect the state as well as *the emancipatory movements themselves* that oppose the state or that take place within it. This is why we have to give up the very general conception of *institution* that we have employed up until this point; it still misses the "principal contradiction." We will return to this in an attempt to examine relationships of institutions and conflict in greater depth. But before then, we should specify what exactly the concrete results have been of the fact that in the modern era the institution developed first and foremost within the form of the nation-state and its various "apparatuses."

State, Representation, Education

If I have not mentioned the *state* very much up until this point, this has not been because I have wished to draw attention away from specifically state institutions, but on the contrary it has been to better illustrate, if possible, what exactly the identification of political institutions with the construction of the nation-state has added to the antinomies of citizenship. Should we believe that subjugating the political to the existence and authority of a state apparatus only ever intensifies these antinomies without changing their nature? Or must we admit that it displaces them onto a whole other field, where the "dialectic" of rights and duties, of ordering and obeying, no longer employs the same terms, such that the categories inherited from ancient political thinking would only serve as masks, as "political fictions"? After Hegel, Marx came quite close to holding this position.

As I've indicated above, the very idea of "constitution" has undergone profound evolutions over the course of its historical development within the national framework, changes that were linked to the growing importance of the state and its control over society, before and after the dominance of the capitalist mode of production, to which it contributed directly through an extremely violent "primitive accumulation" (Marx, 1992 [1867]). The "ancient" constitutions were centered on the distribution of rights among the categories of the populace, rules of exclusion and inclusion, modalities of choice and the responsibility of officeholders, and the definition of powers and counter-powers. They were therefore, in essence, "constitutions in the material sense" that produced a balance of power and lacked the "transcendental neutrality" conferred by the universalization of the legal form. The distinction between a "formal" constitution (founded on the hierarchy of laws, of rules and their origins) and a "material" constitution (balance of power, of social and political bodies, the regulation of conflict between classes and political actors) has a long history that can be traced back to the critiques of "contractualist" theories (Hume, Montesquieu, Hegel), or even further back to debates over "mixed constitutions." In the modern era this distinction has been revisited and defended by Carl Schmitt (2008 [1928]) in particular, as well as some of his interpreters, notably the Italians (Mortati, 1940; Negri, 1999).

In contrast, modern constitutions are "formal constitutions," written in the language of laws, which corresponds – as legal positivism saw – to the autonomization of the state and its monopoly on representing the community, which allows it to exist both "in theory" and "in practice" beyond its divisions and incompleteness (Kelsen, 2013). Modern national constitutionalism therefore combines the *performative declaration* of the universality of rights (along with a legal protection against their violation) with a *new principle* for separating governing from governed that Catherine Colliot-Thélène (2011), in her commentary on the Weberian thesis that bureaucratic legitimacy tends to predominate over other forms of legitimacy, called the principle of *popular ignorance*. We could also say that the institutional version of this idea would be the *incompetence of the people in principle*, whose "capacity to be represented" is its contradictory product. The genealogy of this idea goes all the way back to the representative mechanism for *authorizing the sovereign* as the sole political *actor*, which is the heart of Hobbes' construction in *Leviathan* (1981 [1651], chapters 16 and 17). This was followed by the Hegelian idea according to which the representation of civil society in the state requires the organic intervention of a "universal class" made up of intellectuals who are both public officials as well as spokespeople for societies' interests (Hegel, 1820). This idea is similar to the liberal idea that *property* and *capability* (based on knowledge) are the two sources of "active" citizenship, as Pierre Rosanvallon (1998, 2008), in particular, showed. Closer to the present day, in a more "bourgeois" – and therefore more pragmatic – way, this "incompetence in principle" was systematized by the theoreticians of "elitist democracy" (Schumpeter in particular), who dominated political science at the beginning of the twentieth century (as a reaction to the great "fear of the masses" that was provoked by socialism and communism). They identified "democratic regimes" not only with the delegation of power, but also with competition between political professionals in the "market" of representation.

This shows us just how sharp the contradictions between participation and representation, representation and subordination, must be in modern citizenship, and why the differential of insurrection and constitution has come to focus on national educational systems. Even though they are not blind to its glaring imperfections, many of our contemporaries consider the development of a system of public education to be a democratic achievement and a preliminary condition for the democratization of the citizenry. But we also know that *democracy* and *meritocracy* are in an extremely tense relationship here. The "bourgeois" state that combines political representation with mass education virtually opens itself to the entry of the "common man" or the "everyman" into the political debate and therefore the possibility that he might contest the state's own monopoly on power. To the extent that it is effective in reducing inequalities, it contributes to the inclusion of social categories that have not had access to the public sphere, and therefore the establishment of a "right to rights" (according to Arendt's famous formulation).

Yet let us look at the meritocratic principle that governs these educational systems and that is an integral part of the "educational form" itself – what would a *non-meritocratic* system of universal education look like? Educational utopianism has always pursued this enigmatic goal. The meritocratic principle is already in itself a principle of selecting elites and excluding the multitude from the possibility of truly controlling administrative procedures and participating in public affairs. In any event, the majority of citizens would be incapable of participating *on an equal footing* with the officeholders who have been recruited (and "reproduced") according to their knowledge and ability, whom Pierre Bourdieu called the *state nobility*. By creating a hierarchy of knowledge that is also a hierarchy of power, potentially reinforced by other oligarchical mechanisms, it has *legitimately eliminated* the possibility that the "sovereign nation" could govern itself. It has engaged in a strategic retreat in which "representation" is continually wedded to "elitism" and "demagoguery." We know, moreover, that this was the strong point of the theorizations of the oscillation of mass parties (socialists) between the dictatorship of the leaders and the monopoly of the cadres (Michels, 1915), which Gramsci (1992) responded to with his theory of "organic intellectuals," who would turn the Hegelian idea of the "universal class" and its hegemonic role against the bourgeois state itself.

Democracy and Class Struggle

In mentioning some of the mechanisms that confer a class character on constitutions of citizenship in the modern world, we attempt not only to draw attention to the existence of a gulf between democratic principles and oligarchic realities, but also to raise the question of the way in which "insurrectional" movements have themselves been affected. It is undoubtedly unnecessary to embark on a lengthy justification of the idea that class struggle has played a vital democratic role in the history of modern national citizenship. This is, of course, thanks to the fact that struggles organized by the working class (across the spectrum of their historical forms, from "reformist" to "revolutionary") have led to bourgeois society recognizing and defining certain fundamental *social rights*, the establishment of which the development of industrial capitalism made simultaneously more urgent and more difficult, and which contributed at the same time to the birth of a "social citizenship." But it is also, in a direct relationship with what we have called the legacy of equaliberty, thanks to the fact that class struggles brought together in their own way *individual engagement and collective movements*, a bond which is at the very heart of the idea of insurrection. It is a characteristic trait of modern citizenship, whose value is inextricably both ethical and political, that the *rights of citizens* are carried by individual subjects but conquered through social movements that are able to invent, in each circumstance, the appropriate forms and languages of solidarity. Reciprocally, it is essentially through collective action aiming to conquer or extend rights that the "subjectivization" that autonomizes the individual and grants her a true "power to act" comes. The dominant ideology refuses to acknowledge this, or presents it in inverted form, suggesting that collective political activity is alienating, perhaps even, by its very nature, demeaning or totalitarian.

While resisting this prejudicial view, we should not allow ourselves to be lulled into the illusion either that *organized* class struggles are by nature immune to the internal authoritarianism that stems from their transformation into a "counter-state," and therefore into a counter-power and a counter-violence, or that they represent an unlimited and unconditional principle of universality. It is not happenstance that the majority of the European labor movement and its class organizations remained blind to the problems of colonial oppression, the domestic oppression of women, and the domination exerted over cultural minorities (when the movement itself wasn't directly racist, nationalist, or sexist, of course), and this despite efforts to form an "insurrection within the insurrection." It is not enough to explain this blindness by "material" conditions, or even as a product of "corruption" or a loss of class consciousness. It arises from the fact that resistance and protest against the forms of determined domination or oppression always involve the emergence or construction of *counter-communities* with their own modalities of exclusion and internal hierarchies. In the words of Boaventura de Sousa Santos, one of the foremost theoreticians of *alter-globalization*: "We know that oppression and domination have many faces and that not all of them are the direct or exclusive result of global capitalism. [...] It is, indeed, possible that some initiatives that present themselves as alternatives to global capitalism are themselves a form of oppression" (2005: xxvi). This whole history – often quite dramatic – draws our attention to the *temporality of "insurrectional moments"* – in other words, to the fact that there is no such thing as an "absolutely universal" emancipatory universality that could escape the limitations of its object. The contradictions in the emancipatory politics that call for equaliberty are transposed and reflected inside even the most democratic constitutions, which contributes, at the very least passively, to the possibility of their "de-democratization."

4

From Social Citizenship to the Social-National State

Let us now try to explicate the nexus of the specific contradictions that coalesced around the problem of incorporating "social rights" into citizenship in the twentieth century. It is clear that the importance of the question of social citizenship, of its historical realization and crisis within the framework of the social-national state, is not understood in the same terms in "Northern" and "Southern" political thought. Nonetheless, in the second half of the twentieth century, a counterpart to the social-national state existed in the South in the form of the problematic of "development" (which itself has also been exposed to crisis within the neo-liberal context). Moreover, the question of social rights is not geographically limited to one region of the world. We could argue that – albeit in different ways – it can be felt everywhere that the development of capitalism has resulted in a widening of inequalities. In any event, the critique of formal constitutionalism gives rise to the question of *conflictual democracy*, which must be discussed universally, which is to say, comparatively (Samaddar, 2007).

Let us begin with the relationship between "social citizenship" and the transformations of the representative function of the state, and therefore of modes of organizing the political itself. This question is fascinatingly complex, which is why it has sparked a debate that is still far from being resolved. The recent economic-financial "crisis," and its possible or probable repercussions for the composition of societies and political relationships in the different regions of globalized capitalism, has served in a timely manner to caution us against any hasty or purely speculative conclusions... This debate is especially relevant to interpretations of the transformation in the "class composition" of developed capitalist societies, which had seen the expansion and codification of social rights over the course of the twentieth century, as well as the more or less reversible political consequences of these transformations. It is not easy to say whether "social citizenship," which has only just been recognized and is still far from being generalized, belongs definitively to the past, or to what extent the crisis in which it has been plunged by the development of liberal "globalization" has already destroyed the ability of social systems to resist the development of what Robert Castel (2003, 2009) called *negative forms* of individuality, or *negative individualism*. Nor is it easy to say whether this development coincides with a potentially permanent interruption of the progress of democratization, or, in a more dialectical manner, with an intensification of its internal conflicts and uncertainties, given that it has become increasingly difficult for demands for rights to take the form of collective mass organization.

Can social citizenship, which developed first and foremost in Western Europe (and to a lesser extent in the United States) in the twentieth century, be seen as a potentially universalizable innovation or invention that would belong to the history of citizenship *in general?* This is the question addressed by T.H. Marshall (1950) and his commentators: Sandro Mezzadra (2001, who examines the question of social citizenship within the framework of international migrations) in Italy, as well as Margaret Somers (2008, who combines Marshall's thought with Arendt's notion of the "right to rights") in the United States. Marshall put forward his definition of "social citizenship" in the immediate aftermath of World War II, in the context of a large-scale transformation in the rights of organized labor and in systems for protecting individuals against the risks associated with the "proletarian condition": precariousness and pauperization, exclusion from education and social recognition (which gradually came to affect everyone living off of wage labor, whose livelihoods were not socially guaranteed by income from property).

We must leave this question partly open, because it cannot be answered fully without an analysis of the historical development of capitalism, which is beyond the scope of this work. However, we will assume that, because of the way that it crystallizes a tendency embedded in the very form of the class struggle between capital and labor, there is within the trajectory of social citizenship an irreducible *question* whose scope is general. We could even say that it is the very question of citizenship's "new beginnings" in relation to the "political cycles" of capitalism. The current crisis has amplified this question, and it leads us to look back to the roots of this question in order to envisage possible ways forward. There seem to be three points worth examining here. The first concerns the emergence of social citizenship insofar as it is distinct from a simple *recognition of social rights*, or the granting of a universal dimension to these rights. The second concerns the modality through which the struggles that accompany demands for rights are simultaneously *politicized* and *displaced*, or inscribed into a dynamic of "displaced" class antagonism that authorizes regulation (but can also lead to crisis), by their incorporation into state form (that of the social-national state). The third concerns the complexity of the historical relationships that were then forged between ideas of *socialism* (in the general sense) and *democracy*, whose stakes were above all the representation of "progress" as a political project and the value of "public" action as the modality for establishing the collective. This question has not always been examined in relation to the problems of citizenship (except by "revisionist" socialists such as Eduard Bernstein). It will be up to us to demonstrate as we go why this approach to this question will be the most illuminating.

Social Rights and Social Citizenship

Perhaps the most important aspect of the way in which social citizenship was constituted in the mid-twentieth century is the fact that it was seen not simply as a mechanism for protecting or insuring against the most drastic forms of poverty (or the effects of the *exclusion* of the poor from the possibility of achieving what bourgeois norms considered a "decent" family life, which had been the obsession of nineteenth-century "social criticism"), but rather as a mechanism of *universal solidarity* at the level of the "body politic" and the state. The crucial debate between the "particularist" and paternalist conception and the universalist egalitarian conception has been summarized quite well by the historians of social democracy (Sassoon, 1996). This debate was the culmination of fierce controversies that dated back to the Industrial Revolution arguments over the connection between philanthropy and bourgeois strategies for *disciplining* the labor force. In *The Birth of Biopolitics* (2008), Foucault reminded us that in the polemics surrounding the "Beveridge plan" of 1942, precursors of neo-liberalism like Friedrich Hayek (*The Road to Serfdom*, 1944) conflated the plan with Nazism. It remains to be seen whether similarly violent counterarguments will emerge around the "citizen's income" that certain contemporary theorists argue should be instituted as a response to generalized "precariousness" and as a way to actualize the distinction between social rights and the assignment of specific professional identities to individuals.

The mechanism of solidarity that was established to varying extents by the welfare state concerned virtually every citizen and covered all of society, which is to say, the rich and the poor had *equal right* to it. This point is symbolic, but also economically crucial. Rather than saying that the poor were, from then on, treated like the rich, it is more accurate to say that the rich were *treated like the poor*, on the basis of the universalization of the anthropological category of "labor" as the uniquely human trait. The majority of the "social rights" guaranteed or conferred by the state were effectively conditioned by the more or less stable engagement of "active" individuals in professions that gave them a *status* recognized by society as a whole. In a certain sense, work replaced family (or, at least, competed with it) as the "foundation" of society. This point is also essential to explaining why it is that we speak of *social citizenship*, including a democratic component, and not simply "social democracy." Class divisions persist, of course, and capital (whether private or public) retains control of the operations of production and investment. We can take note that one of the sharpest problems posed by the extension of citizenship that accompanied this anthropological revolution relates to the equality of the sexes, given the fact that the majority of women in Europe and the United States in the mid-twentieth century were still "socialized" to be the *spouses of active "laborers,"* and therefore subjugated to them. Access to professional activity became a key path for the emancipation of women. But it also led to the overexploitation of women, through the creation of the "double work day," both professional and domestic; as well as their creation as a minority group through "female professions," such as schoolteacher, nurse, secretary, and so on, which reproduced segregation within the public space – what Geneviève Fraisse (2001) called the system of "two governments."

It is also important to note the more or less indirect economic and ideological ties that connected social protection and the prevention of precariousness (which Marx considered one of the central characteristics of the "proletarian condition") with a political agenda of *reducing inequalities*. These were so powerfully bound together that, up until the emergence of "neo-liberalism," no "party" could try to disentangle them, at least openly. This political agenda included developing "equality of opportunity" and increasing individual social mobility through the extension of the access of *future* citizens to the educational system (in other words, the symbolic dismantling or delegitimizing of the cultural monopoly of the bourgeoisie, which had guaranteed its exclusive access to *capacities*, in addition to *property*) and the establishment of *progressive taxation*, applied to income both from labor and from capital. Classical capitalism had completely omitted this "redistributive" mechanism, which, as we know, is being increasingly eroded today, and this has led to what has been called the "fiscal crisis of the state" (O'Connor, 1973), in turn used to "justify" the limitation or elimination of social rights.

These co-occurrences are why the new political system that was gradually established (in a close relationship with "social democratic" agendas, even when "right-wing" governments were in power) cannot be reduced to an enumerated list of *social rights*, and even less to a paternalist system of "social protections" conferred from on high to "vulnerable" individuals, who are perceived as *passive beneficiaries of social aid* (even if liberal ideologues do not tire of presenting it in this manner and drawing the conclusion that it is necessary to be eternally vigilant against the "abuses" of social security and to "manage" the distribution of funds with "thrift"). The whole question lies in understanding what remains of this universalism today, given that not only are its principles under fire from neo-liberal theorists, but it is also being undermined by two correlative phenomena: the relativization of the national borders inside of which this universalism had been progressively established (in certain "Northern" countries) – with the result that workers must now compete against one another across the globe – and the destabilization of the professional relationship between work and individuality (or, to put it another way, the retreat of the anthropological category of "activity" as the foundation of social *recognition* in favor of "entrepreneurship" and "communication," perhaps even "care").

Material Constitutions

The institutions of social citizenship have rendered the ensemble of social rights, which it legitimated as "fundamental rights," a fluctuating reality, one that is even more fragile than other democratic acquisitions, because it depended on a historical power struggle and was therefore subject to alternating fits and starts, advances and retreats, against the backdrop of a *structural asymmetry* between the power of capital and that of labor, an asymmetry whose resolution was never truly on the table. We can note that in none of the Western European countries that were at one moment or another governed by social democratic parties was the complete system of social rights ever inscribed as a "basic norm" in Kelsen's (2013) sense, which is to say, at the core of a formal constitution guaranteeing "basic rights." This observation should, of course, be nuanced relative to the specific cases of different nations. The post-war French and Italian constitutions (1945) included a reference to labor rights and social protection within the context of an expanded conception of "public power." The case of the United Kingdom is unique because even though it lacks a written constitution, this novel conception of citizenship was taken further there than anywhere else. The German case is particularly complex and interesting. "Social politics" date back to Bismarck and, passing through the tragic vicissitudes of the Weimar Republic, Nazism, and the partition of the country into two opposing "blocs" during the Cold War, it divides social citizenship between a model of a liberal "co-management" of capitalism and a model of "authoritarian socialism."

This is why we must once again appeal to the idea of a "material constitution" as applied to citizenship, one that establishes a balance of powers between social classes that is indirectly sanctioned by the law (or more generally by the *norm*) at different levels, but that essentially represents a contingent co-occurrence of rights and social movements that are themselves more or less institutionalized. There is undoubtedly a considerable kernel of truth to the idea, which is widely held among Marxists, that the "Keynesian compromise" consisted in trading the recognition of social rights and the institutional representation of the labor movement in regulatory bodies in exchange for moderating working class demands for higher wages and abandoning the perspective of the overthrow of capitalism (and that thus in a way it represented the *end of the proletariat* in the "subjective" sense, the one that for Marx involved the revolutionary idea and project). As Keynes himself saw, the necessary conditions for this compromise were both *internal* to "developed" capitalist countries and *external* (or geopolitical), insofar as they arose from the "fear of communism" that gripped the Western bourgeoisies after the October 1917 revolution and the establishment of "socialism in a single country."

The result of this historical bargain was the long-pursued goal of a relative neutralization of the violence of social conflict, but that was only one side of the coin. Today, with the passage of time and in light of the contrast provided by a new cycle of proletarianization (which Castel, Negri, and others have called the emergence of the *precariat,* a portmanteau of precarious and proletariat), in which the disequilibrium of social forces at the global level is compounded by the ossification of the system of social citizenship, we can see that these struggles did not disappear purely and simply. From this point of view it is especially important to underline the *heterogeneity* of the "'68 moment" and its "anti-systemic" dimension in addition to its "anti-authoritarian" transversality (Wallerstein et al., 1989). The great class struggles of the 1970s marked the beginning of the end of this "equilibrium," at the same time as technology was being revolutionized and we were moving closer to the hegemony of financial capitalism – even before the collapse of "real socialism" and the acceleration of economic globalization. But it is also clear that the violence of these struggles tended to be displaced onto other battlefields, avoiding direct political confrontation between classes: war between nations, postcolonial "culture" clashes, and Durkheimian social "anomie," which is to say the individual or collective "irrational" violence that accompanies the imposition of any "micropolitical" system of norms for morality and rational behavior.

It is at an even more general level that we should examine the functioning of social citizenship under the sign of a *displacement of antagonism,* operated by (and, for a time, to the benefit of) the social-national state. The characteristic phenomenon of the self-limitation of the violence of struggles (in which we can see the effects of bourgeois *civility*) can be explained by the relative effectiveness of a model of political organization that combines "parliamentary" and "extra-parliamentary" action. But in turn, this model can only be understood within the framework of a dual displacement over time, embedded within the necessary preconditions of the political system:

1   The displacement of definitions of "fundamental rights" away from the sphere of labor in the strict sense, or – in Marxist terms – away from the sphere of *production* towards that of the *reproduction of the labor force* (which is to say, the forms and conditions of individual or family existence, which today we call *soin* or "care," but that formerly we spoke of as service). The latter can, in fact, be the object of a consensual normalization, while with regard to the former this could only be accomplished with great difficulty, or in the context of an ever-precarious power struggle. This is why it is crucial to think about the way in which the struggles over labor organization, "Taylorist" forms of authority, collective resistance by laborers to the capitalist atomization of the labor force, developed *before 1968 and afterwards*. Capital has definitively destabilized the power struggle in its own favor by launching "globalization from below," which is to say, by resorting on a massive scale to the labor of immigrants and groups marginalized or excluded by the historical working-class organizations, within the framework of "postcolonial" competition. From this standpoint, anti-imperialist decolonization itself became functional.

2   The displacement of social antagonism onto the level of *international* relations between state systems. The division of the world into two camps during the "Cold War" had an ambiguous effect here. On the one hand, it linked the struggles for social rights to a real or imagined "danger": a Soviet-style revolution in the West, carried out not only by industrial laborers, but also by the peasants, workers, and intellectuals who had been ideologically won over by communism. This incited the political representatives of national capitalism to seek out a compromise with organized labor and, more generally, to develop their own model of "social progress" (following the advice of Keynes, Roosevelt, and other historical "strategists" of the bourgeoisie). On the

other hand, it allowed for the creation of an ideological rift within the labor movement, between communism and anti-communism, which would pick up on and incorporate other divisions (between secular and Christian labor unionism, skilled and unskilled laborers, nationals and immigrants, etc.). Of course, the increasingly visible anti-democratic nature of the Soviet system did a great deal to accentuate this rift.

With the end of the Cold War and the acceleration of financial globalization, *social fear "changed sides"*; it is no longer the capitalists who are afraid of the revolution, but workers who are afraid of unemployment and competition by immigrants. This is how the power struggle that had been the "external" foundation for the social-national state was destabilized at the same time as the limits of its "universalism" were beginning to appear from within.

National and Democratic Socialism

This quite schematic overview of the historical problems that can be linked to the category of "social citizenship" brings us back to the characteristic tension of conflict and the institution. It is this tension that expresses the persistence of a political dimension, *the continuation by other means* of the dialectic of insurrection and constitution. As undeniably real as the moral and social concerns of the bourgeoisie might have been, it is altogether insufficient to portray the emergence of social citizenship as a philanthropic concession made by the bourgeois state under the guise of "repairing" the pathological effects of the Industrial Revolution and unrestrained capitalist exploitation, or even as the logical consequence of capitalism's need to regulate the free reign of the market, which threatened to destroy the moral and physical integrity of the labor force upon which it depended for the production of surplus value. This is perhaps the limitation of Robert Castel's analyses, which are fundamentally grounded on a sociological (Durkheimian) conception of society as an organism confronting the processes of disaggregation and anomie created by untamed capitalism, and as such emphasize the "regulatory reaction" of public power and minimize the dynamic of class conflict, and therefore the labor movement's specific contribution to the institution of social citizenship. It is true that orthodox Marxism, for its part, denies the very possibility that the class struggle could be balanced through a "constitutional" approach. There are, of course, some notable exceptions to this, such as Nicos Poulantzas in France and Claus Offe in Germany, but they are precisely not "orthodox Marxists."

There is therefore no doubt that the two factors given above had an impact upon the transformations of the contents of citizenship in the "developed" capitalist countries where organized class struggles took place. However, a third element in competition with the other two was required in order to provoke their combination. Today, we can now argue that *this element was "socialism,"* in the diversity of its different strains, formulations, and organizations. Socialism is not simply an ideology, much less a theoretical doctrine. It is a complex historical institution that, in the nineteenth and twentieth centuries, fanned out into several strands: *conservative* or authoritarian socialism (whose realized form we would see in the single-party states of the communist bloc), *reformist* socialism (or social democracy), and *utopian* or *messianic* socialism (generally in the form of a critique of the earlier two, with either a Christian or liberation foundation).

The states that established social citizenship to varying degrees of completeness should be historically defined as *states that were at once both "national" and "social."* This should be understood as meaning that their programs for social reforms were by definition designed and implemented within national borders, under the auspices of national sovereignty (which means that they could not have existed without a sufficient degree of autonomy and economic independence). However, reciprocally, the nation-state could overcome its own contradictions, both internal and external, *only by universalizing social rights.* This was especially true in moments of acute crisis, when the political as such vacillated, as was the case in the context of "total war" in the twentieth century. It was essentially the experience of war that, in Europe, brought the labor movement over the crucial threshold with regard to representativeness and ability to negotiate. Though it had long been a key demand of the labor movement, the declaration of social rights as "fundamental rights" only came in the aftermath of the two world wars in which workers killed each other by the millions... There is a deep irony or "cunning of history" at work here, as the initial aim of European socialism had been to prevent the war.

This is how the nexus between the two attributes of the state (the "national" and the "social") came into existence, leading each one to become in practice a necessary precondition of the other. But we must take this one step further. The "socialist" element in modern politics embodied, albeit only in part and for a certain time, the "insurrectional" side of citizenship. It therefore also carried with it a tendency towards radical democracy. When it found itself integrated into the horizon of *nationalism*, it did not simply dissolve into it leaving behind no residue – except when the confluence of a serious social and moral crisis gave rise to a "totalitarian" discourse and politics.

It is this *distance* or this *difference*, which is maintained at the core of the social-national state, that made it possible – for a time – for the socialism born in the nineteenth century to contribute to the formation of a *public and political sphere*, one that was relatively autonomous with respect to both the state, with its parliamentary institutions, and "civil society," with its marketplace and contractual operations. In this sense, "socialism" is the common envelope for a whole series of evolving contradictions. Having never reached its "final goal" of passing beyond capitalism, it remained a project or a program for reforms that were contested both internally and externally. But, as an "aspirational horizon" internalized by the multitude, it never ceased to create conflict within the institution that joined together capital and labor, private property and solidarity, market and state rationality. It also contributed to the "public" sphere becoming a "political" sphere in a strong sense. Oskar Negt and Alexander Kluge gave a radical interpretation of this antinomy in their landmark book on the political *experience* of the labor movement (*Public Sphere and Experience*, 1993), a response to Habermas' theory of the bourgeois public sphere. This was only the case within certain limits, however, because, as we have said, social citizenship needed to tie itself to the reproduction of capitalist relationships of property, and political struggles needed to inscribe themselves within the framework of a relative neutralization of antagonisms. This meant that the state was equipped with mechanisms for reproducing political *consensus*, and that it restrained adversaries from turning into enemies (even if this meant a return to direct repression when worker "autonomy" became too great to be controlled at the scale of society as a whole). This also meant that "society" had to be reconfigured as a process for the generalized normalization of individual behavior. But at the same time the system tended to crystallize the social power struggle and establish it within a compromise that would end up seeming untenable to both "dominant" and "dominated" alike.

The Antinomy of Progress

This is a good point of departure if we wish to understand what today appears to be a true *antinomy of progress*, for which the history of social citizenship is an almost perfect illustration. Only the perspective of limitless progress, which is to say, the idealized collective desire to attain an effective *equality of opportunity* for every individual in society, could have controlled the pressures that would otherwise have tended to erode privileges and kept inveterate forms of domination at bay, expanding the space of freedoms for the multitude. The limits to progress were nonetheless inscribed in the material constitution that brought together the national and the social, the reproduction of capacities for capital accumulation and the generalization of social rights, the ethos of collective action and a "majoritarian" conformism. The democratic conquests that took place within the framework of the social-national state were quite real, and they gave rise to many "progressive" moments over the course of its construction (sometimes in quasi-insurrectional ways, such as the *Front Populaire*). But they were always followed by a reaffirmation of structural limits, in the form of creeping counter-reforms or more violent repression.

It will be decisive to our analysis of the current crisis in the very idea of "social citizenship" itself, as well as the various forms taken by the planned dismantling of the social state, for us to understand what has caused this crisis, which has had an impact on employment security and universal healthcare, the democratization of access to higher education, the domestic and professional liberation of women, and finally the principle of representation itself. Is it chiefly the result of an attack launched by capitalism "from the outside," based on the demands of an increasingly trans-nationalized economy, where the logic of finance has won out over the logic of industry? Or is it the result of "internal" contradictions within social citizenship, and the fact that it is reaching its own historical limits? The perspective of a *continual progression* down the path of fundamental rights (Stourzh, 1989), especially with regard to the link between individual autonomy and solidarity, runs up against not only the interests of dominant social groups and the system of "exploitation" that it opposes, but also its own immanent limitations.

We can advance the idea that the socialism of the nineteenth and twentieth centuries was the prisoner of a fusion between *progressivism* and *statism*. It was caught in the aporia of "conflictual democracy," to which we shall return; it cannot be disassociated either from the permanence of conflict, or from the institutionalization of its forces, of its organizations and its discourses as components of a "public" sphere identified with the national community. The result is altogether paradoxical from the point of view of a Marxian topography of the political. Yet its nature also allows it to outflank liberal "critiques"; the *politicization* of social questions, which is denounced as a degradation of the autonomy of the political by "neo-republicans," even those who, like Arendt, are hostile to capitalism, does not abolish the dualism of the "political" and the "police" (Rancière, 1999), but rather strengthens it. This has had the specific result that the expansion of the domains of political invention and intervention is not taking place so much on the side of labor, to which rights remain symbolically attached, as on the side of "reproduction": family, culture, public services. It is to this side that the neo-liberal offensive will turn, after it has broken the resistance of labor in the domains of production through a combination of new technologies, the mobility of labor across borders, and the "individualization" of professions – the trend by which tasks are becoming less and less "collective" and are increasingly assigned to individual workers, in a way that makes unified resistance more difficult.

As we can see, this hypothesis with dialectical aspirations does not fail to consider social antagonisms, but it draws us away from the picture of a conspiracy of malevolent capitalists (or a variant that is very popular in "Latin" Europe: the "Anglo-Saxon model" of corporate capitalism). It is also more *political*, in the sense that it proposes frameworks of intelligibility that feature not only structures, but also collective action. The working classes in the "North," who benefited from important social conquests (as *wage-earning* classes) and who today find their security and mobility gradually slipping away, do not appear in this account as *victims* alone. They are and always have been, to a certain extent, *actors*, whose ability to determine their own history has depended on shifting internal and external conditions, in particular the way in which they have *represented themselves* in the systems in which they act, and the collectivities that have empowered them in practice. This hypothesis is the one that we have been looking for. It will allow us to examine some of the features of what is today called "neoliberalism." This examination will be based on the interpretation put forward by Wendy Brown in her 2003 essay "Neo-liberalism and the End of Liberal Democracy," whose influence has been widely felt in the contemporary debates within the "critical" political theory movement. Before we do this, however, we should pause, in the wake of this first series of genealogical investigations, to examine and illustrate two general questions: first, the relationship between *citizenship and exclusion*, and then the question of *conflictual democracy*, which we have already touched on several times.

5

Citizenship and Exclusion

If it were true that a constituent tension between the categories of democracy and citizenship traverses the entire history of the political institution, it would seem as if such a configuration would always lead to a discussion of exclusion from citizenship (with regard to slaves, women, wage laborers, and colonial subjects, as discussed previously). And also, it seems that more work needs to be done before we can enter into a *general* analysis of this question, as this description does not offer a clear answer to the question of whether we are dealing with an arbitrary grouping of independent and heterogeneous historical "cases," or whether, on the contrary, what we are seeing is the same characteristic returning and changing positions from one social structure to another. Moreover, it is true that – for reasons worth exploring – in contemporary discussions of politics in the "post-national" or "post-liberal" era, the category of exclusion has tended to supplant that of inequality and become generalized, which has had the effect of both obscuring questions of citizenship and rendering them concrete.

Here, we will turn our attention specifically to the paradoxical relationship that emerges in the modern era between the concept of *universalized* citizenship – both in the sense of one that is founded on universal principles and in the sense of one that spans distinctions of political regime and cultural tradition – and certain forms of *internal exclusion*. From the perspective of defining citizenship, these forms will appear either contradictory or constituent. Abolishing them would therefore require more than simply lifting restrictions on the application of a right; it would necessitate transforming the interpretation of the principles of citizenship themselves.

Exclusion, Inequalities, Discriminations

These debates over exclusion from citizenship are not new. Rancière (1999: 116) quotes Bonald as saying that "certain persons are in society without being of society." I could not have put it better myself. Over the last decade, these debates have forcefully re-emerged in the West in the wake of the riots in the cities of the "North" and "South" (notably Paris and London) that were provoked or facilitated by ethnic segregation in the urban "*banlieues*" and "ghettos" (Balibar 2013). Sociological generalization is always controversial, of course. In his analysis of the 2005 riots, Robert Castel (2007) expressed the opinion that the term "exclusion" was ill suited to the circumstances, because the unemployed youth of African or North African descent who clashed with police were French citizens in the legal sense of the term. He preferred the category "negative discrimination." Loïc Wacquant (2004), for his part, maintained that the "*banlieues*" were not ghettos in the American sense, to the extent that communities of foreign descent do not represent a historically separate space in the "city." Castel then wrote:

> No more than the *banlieue* is not a ghetto, the young immigrant in the *banlieue* is not "excluded," at least, so long as

we wish for the term to retain a specific meaning. Exclusion
in the strict sense implies a division of the population into
two strict categories, placing the "excluded" outside of the
functioning of society, having neither the rights nor the
ability and resources necessary to play a role in the collectiv-
ity. [...] the youth in the *banlieues* nonetheless still enjoy
several prerogatives that accompany belonging to the French
nation: public citizenship and social citizenship. Independent
of their ethnic origins, the majority of the young people in
the "projects" in the *banlieues* are French citizens, and therefore in principle they enjoy political rights and equality
before the law, at least once they become adults. Tocqueville
often said that civic rights represent a form of nobility conferred on the people as such. We know that it took centuries
of struggle to obtain these rights, and even then they were
not extended to everyone right away. It was only in 1945
that women received the right to vote in France, significantly
later than in most other industrialized nations. (Castel,
2007: 34)

Therefore, the young French citizens of immigrant descent
are not strictly speaking *excluded*, because even though they
are the targets of *discrimination* based on class, race, and
age, they still enjoy the fundamental rights that, as a whole,
constitute "social citizenship."

But even Castel had to recognize that there is a risk of
confusion here. It is undoubtedly true that in comparison to
other populations in other areas of the world who are threatened by famine or deportation these young "immigrants"
remain relatively protected from social risks. Even from a
cultural perspective, they are not strictly speaking outside of
society; on the contrary, they contribute to the creation of a
"hybrid culture" within it. But even while an argument like
this cautions us against using the term "exclusion" in a vague
and emphatic manner – directed particularly at those who
suggest that the contradictions of contemporary citizenship

simply reproduce the age-old oppositions between "citizens" and "subjects" in colonial empires – nonetheless, it does not erase the *structural* nature of these contradictions. We can turn to the comparison, which Castel himself uses, of what, several years earlier, Geneviève Fraisse, in a discussion of the situation of women in the republican space, called "exclusionary democracy" (Fraisse, 2001). She traced its genealogy all the way back to the conflicts during the French Revolution over the relegation of women to "passive citizenship," as opposed to the "active citizenship" of men (which coincided with the establishment of popular representation as the foundation of the state), the consequences of which would continue to be felt even after the formal ascension of women to "equal" citizenship. The fact that this discrimination was embedded in the heart of political institutions for so long has left a deep scar, particularly in the form of a rigid separation between the "public" sphere and the "domestic" sphere, which assigned each gender a different social role, and denied women the ability to govern (offering them, "in compensation," "governance of the home"). This was not external exclusion in the strict sense, but rather internal exclusion, and this concept did not consist in the legal status of women on its own, but its combination with representations and practices as well. The importance of formal rights is undeniable, but their relationship with the use and distribution of power, with "empowerment," is no less so.

The Question of the "Right to Rights"

It is in this sense that we can propose expanding Arendt's idea of a "right to rights" – on the condition, of course, that we go beyond her arbitrarily imposed limits. In fact, for quite some time now, the political use of this idea has extended beyond its strictly statutory definition. It has shifted from a "constituted power" (the right to rights is the result

of belonging to an existing political community, particularly
a nation-state) to a "constituent power," the active ability to
assert rights in a public space or, better yet, dialectically, the
possibility of *not being excluded from the right to fight for
one's rights*. And this is precisely the obstacle that confronts
many social groups, even in our most liberal "democracies."
They experience the fluctuating line between "resistance"
(which we could call the *minimal right*) and "exclusion"
(which is rightlessness). Specifically, if there were no resistance, in its diverse forms (which are not necessarily violent),
they could find themselves completely excluded, "displaced"
outside of the territories in which they had acquired formal
rights, legal protections, returned to territories where there
is no active citizenship, at times to situations where even
freedom and survival themselves are precarious. And, in
fact, it is sometimes within these very democracies, in refugee
"camps" or in communities of "illegal" immigrants (Caloz-
Tschopp, 2004), that we find these social groups. More
often, however, we find them *on the boundaries* themselves,
in the places where the question is precisely the possibility
of expression or assertion, and therefore of *political existence*. This was, in fact, exactly the scope of Arendt's thinking about the condition of "stateless" individuals and
collectivities, on the basis of which she elaborated her idea
of the "right to rights."

Existence in the form of resistance is not always possible,
or rather it is not always possible without recourse to anti-
institutional violence that aims to "break down the gates"
of the space of citizenship and social recognition. But these
very same violent protests can end up being completely coun-
ter-productive because of an overwhelming dissymmetry of
forces, which will have the negative result of reinforcing the
feeling among the "excluded" that they do not belong. In the
case of the urban riots, which were primarily undertaken by
youths, class and race discrimination mutually reinforced

one another. The former took the form of what has been ironically called "preferential unemployment," the alienating choice between unemployment and precariousness that is in the process of reconstituting a *proletariat* in the traditional sense. The latter came in the form of a "genealogical framework" that continues to treat the descendants of immigrants as foreigners (or "immigrants"), in flagrant contradiction of republican law. On top of these there are the effects of a collective imagination that portrays the young immigrant as a potential domestic enemy, who threatens not only the community's security, but also its cultural and religious identity (including when the official religious identity is "secularism"). The combined effect of these internal class and race exclusions offers a perfect illustration of what Castel himself defined as the *negative individualism* that arises from the dismantling of the social-national state by neo-liberal policies: a situation in which individuals are exhorted to behave as "entrepreneurs" of their own lives, constantly pursuing maximal efficiency, while at the same time being deprived of the social conditions that would allow them to assert their autonomy. I should add to this that if there are forms of *negative individuality*, then there are also, it would seem, forms of *negative community* that emerge once, in the mimetic circle, the revolt against violence and exclusion itself takes on violent forms that neutralize its effectiveness, and that the dominant system can easily manipulate and exploit in order to justify its own security policies. "Post-colonial" France, and Europe in general, provide us with a typical illustration of this: we find, at the same time, the legacy of centuries-old discrimination against the "subjects" of colonial domination, now transformed more or less completely into class differences, along with new varieties of "passive citizenship" that have resulted from the weakening of social movements and their ability to "transform society." The category of exclusion thus remains irremediably complex and heterogeneous, but it also represents a place that is strategically overdetermined by the current contradictions of citizenship.

Politics and Territoriality: Borders

We must now take a theoretical detour that will enable us to both understand the philosophical dimensions of the idea of internal exclusion and inscribe them within a teleology of citizenship as a form of the political. We will be looking for a working hypothesis that would enable us to understand what would justify (and on what terms) expanding the category of exclusion to the point that it would encompass all the phenomena of the denial of citizenship, ranging from *discrimination* to *elimination*.

To do this, it would not be a bad idea to begin by explicating the underlying territorial metaphor. As has been emphasized by Gilles Deleuze and Félix Guattari (1987), on the one hand, and Carlo Galli (2010), on the other – although they approached it from very different perspectives – all political practice is *territorialized*. It identifies or classifies individuals and populations relative to their ability to occupy a space, or be admitted to it. Yet incorporation to a territory has as a quasi-transcendental condition of possibility the existence of a situation of mutual *recognition* of individuals and groups, either in the sense of belonging to the same "community," or in the sense of participating in "commerce," which is to say, in communication and exchange, even, at the extremes, a sense of confrontation within the same conflict or the same "struggle." Because of this dual determination, through territory as well as recognition, exclusion as a general political phenomenon has a status that is very close to that of the *border*, which isolates or protects communities, but which also makes communication possible and crystallizes conflicts. Like the border, within the political field exclusion represents a quintessentially two-sided phenomenon, both historical and symbolic. To this extent it is also deeply *amphibological*, meaning that the two sides never cease interfering with one another. The empirical, historical, phenomena of territorialization and de-territorialization (such as the displacement of populations, migrations, the fortification of borders, barriers to communication) are transformed into determinations of the universal, which is to say, into regimes of rights and access to rights. Distinctions that emerged from the universe of symbolism, such as "anthropological differences" of gender, age, culture, which as a whole characterize humanity as a "species," are transformed into (more or less constraining) material instruments for assigning individuals and groups to territories and regulating their circulation. Here we have touched upon the fundamental epistemological fact that spatial categories such as territory, residence, ownership of land, but also, correlatively, travel, nomadism, and sedentariness, are also constituent determinations of citizenship. We must therefore incorporate into our definition of the political institution the fact that these cycle in an unpredictable manner between the empirical and the transcendental, the historical and the symbolic.

These remarks are abstract, but their implications are immediate when we turn to the phenomenon of *internal exclusion*. In its most general definition, it means that an "external" border is mirrored by an "internal" border, or that the condition of foreignness is projected within a political space or national territory to create an inadmissible alterity (as was the case with slaves and is the case with immigrants), or, on the contrary, an additional element of interiority and belonging is introduced into an anthropological category, in such a way as to push the foreigner out (as is the case whenever women are appropriated as bearers of the national identity and held responsible for the reproduction of its "purity"). In both cases, "other spaces," or "heterotopias", as Foucault would say, disrupt the homogeneity of the communal space, or, on the contrary, reinforce it, by marking the exceptional position occupied by the *other man* and guarding against him symbolically and institutionally. In practice, this can only take place through the emergence of rules of inclusion and exclusion. It is at the level of these rules (which are partly implicit and partly explicit) that we must ask the always difficult questions about continuities and variations among the figures of the stranger, the pariah, the monster, the "sub-human," the internal enemy, the exile...

Starting from here we can now return from a critical angle to the ideas of belonging and being-in-common that have been presupposed by the idea of citizenship dating back to its ancient iterations, but which have also never stopped mutating. It seems self-evident that *political exclusion* (or *politicized* exclusion) is the other side of the constitution of an *exclusive community*. But the diversity among the examples we would have to consider is daunting; some of them do not exhibit a conspicuous form of separation of a form akin to a border. Take, for example, being excluded from "commerce" itself, or from communication, translation, mobility – phenomena that in the contemporary world, characterized by the intensification of the exchange of information, the circulation of goods and people, seem just as discriminatory as being refused admission to a certain territory or being expelled from it. These terms do not reflect the static phenomena of the existence of political communities and their historical relationships with determined territories, so much as a second-degree phenomenon, a more dynamic one. This would be the *relationship* between communities, the *exchange* of goods, and of the signs and individuals that reciprocally constitute these communities, as well as the varying degrees of "freedom" that this exchange confers upon individuals with respect to community *belonging*, between the two extreme poles of immutable *adherence* and voluntary *adhesion*. Therefore, these terms testify, albeit often in the register of alienation and violence, to the fact that the existence of political communities implies not only a relationship *to themselves*, a principle of belonging or a right to participate in collective life, but also an *external* recognition of and by the other, with or without perfect reciprocity.

This consideration is obviously crucial for understanding the sense in which modern nation-states, in order to affirm their character as "sovereign" political communities, needed not only to maintain relationships of "commerce" with one another and to establish an "international law" that would govern times of war and peace, but also to use this dual foundation to construct a "cosmopolitanism" of a new type, endowed with a meta-legal role (as we see in particular with the account given by Kant [1983 (1796)]). The "citizen of the world" (*Weltbürger*) was the concrete counterpart (as a merchant, as an "intellectual" in the *République des Lettres*, perhaps even as a politico-religious exile or "refugee") of the legal constitution of the nation-states (what Schmitt [2003 (1950)] called the *Ius Publicum Europaeum*, one of whose preconditions was European dominance and the division of the world among the various colonial powers). This world citizen was not an imaginary member of a *civitas* or a *polis* without boundaries, whose limits would coincide with the expansion of the universe; on the contrary, he was a *being in relationship* who circulated (or not) between territories and states. It is on this basis that we should ask what the contradictory results – what new possibilities for recognition, what new internal and external violences – have been of the contemporary transformations of "trade" and "international law," now that the movements of populations, the dispersion of cultural communities, and the postcolonial flow of populations in the reverse direction have become mass phenomena.

Rules of Inclusion, Rules of Exclusion

If it is true, as a result, that, in their relationship to territory as to the more abstract "political space" that forms the horizon of citizenship, there still remains this problematic reciprocity between belonging and commerce, being in common and being in relationship, then we should think about inclusion and exclusion as indicators of the essential instability of the community of citizens, which is constantly calling for new "guarantees" that themselves put the community at risk, and of the fact that its conditions of possibility are always infinitesimally close to its conditions of impossibility. More precisely, we can formulate *three theses* concerning inclusion and exclusion in general:

First Thesis   There can be no institutional procedure for exclusion without a *rule*, whether it be a rule of law or a practical, sociological, norm. But the exclusionary rule must be the inverse of a rule or normative system of inclusion – thus the strategic scope of the ideas of belonging and participation, what political scientists with their characteristic cynicism call admission to the citizenship "club." It is important to keep in mind this necessary co-occurrence of rules (or norms) for inclusion and exclusion, so that we do not forget that violence, which is always present in these matters, is not situated on the side of exclusion alone. *Inclusion itself can be just as violent*, whether it takes the form of forced (or at least coerced, under pain of "social death") "conversion" or assimilation. The *compelle eos intrare* did not disappear with the ebbing of the political power of churches to "compel adhesion for the purpose of salvation," which Saint Augustine based on a line from the Gospel – it has only taken other, more "secular" and more "everyday" forms. Cultural anthropology has taught us how to discern the element of violence, whether consciously organized or not, that resides not only in all processes of colonization (whether internal or external), but also in acculturation and therefore in education, insofar as education is the assimilation of individuals into a socially "dominant" or "common" culture.

In truth, we must account for a *dual violence* inherent in the necessary co-occurrence of inclusions and exclusions. Therefore we must look at the problem of the "civilization" of civilization itself, or of a civilization that morally and politically confronts its own "discontent" (Freud), its own element of violence or savagery. From this standpoint we can posit that *citizenship* is a political regulation of this violence and that it concedes a space of varying size to it, but that it never suppresses it purely and simply. It is evidently crucial to analyze and evaluate the forms this takes, which can be more or less symmetrical. It could be that the conditions that define belonging also *ipso facto* identify non-belonging (as in the ideal scenario of a relationship between "us" and "them"). One could imagine that, in modern states, "nationality" functions in this simple way, that in one swoop it instituted the equivalence between *citizenship and nationality* that we earlier called "foundational." But things are more complicated in practice, because within active citizenship there are many degrees (even in places that officially do not recognize the categories of "reduced" or "second-class" citizens that characterized the apartheid regime and colonization in general). Above all there is a *gray area* where individuals are neither completely included nor completely excluded (just as there are "foreigners who cannot be legally expelled" from a given territory, because of family ties, for instance, but who nonetheless "cannot become legal residents"). This boils down to saying that the rules of inclusion are not purely and simply the inverse of the rules of exclusion. Thus, the constituent relationship between community and exclusion can begin to function *in the opposite direction*; instead of a pre-existing definition of community, predisposed to make the simple differentiation between citizen and non-citizen, reality is created out of an *unresolved conflict*, one which never stops evolving, which for the most part takes place "behind the scenes" of citizenship (or on *another stage* of the political), and whose stakes are discriminatory violence, inequalities in statuses and rights, whose anthropological "material" is sexual, racial, religious, cultural…Through this conflict, the institutional community is mirrored by an "imagined community" (Anderson, 1983), just as the external border comes to be mirrored by an internal border (Fichte, 2008 [1808]), but it is also *politically transformed*, whether it be in the direction of restriction or expansion.

Second Thesis   One consequence that follows from this and that is far from purely speculative, but rather applies to the daily political experience, is that exclusion and inclusion do not describe fixed rules or situations so much as the stakes of the conflicts through which citizenship, in a sense, "thinks" its own conditions of possibility. If someone is excluded from citizenship in a radical manner, particularly if this is done through what we have called "internal exclusion," this never means that she simply remains outside of the community, like a foreigner who can be refused a visa or denied naturalization (which, as we know, is always applied *differentially*). It means that she is *excluded from inclusion*, in other words, from a status, but also, at a deeper level, from a power or capacity. Arendt's formula of the "right to rights" does not reflect the *institution* of citizenship so much as *the access to citizenship*, or, better yet, *citizenship as access* and as an ensemble of procedures for access (Van Gunsteren, 1998).

We must then understand this concept of "right to rights" as a unity of opposites in the dialectical sense. Arendt herself, given the circumstances (and the tenuous analogies that she attempted to develop between the different types of domination and elimination that were characteristic of modernity), focused mostly on developing the *negative side*: the fact that "stateless" individuals are deprived of the fundamental right (or "personhood") that is the precondition of all others. But there is also the *positive* or, better yet, the *affirmative side*: the side that we saw when we defined "active citizenship" as a form of participation that already manifests itself in demands for access (or belonging). In these cases it is not founded on an existing right, but constitutes one or imposes its recognition. Symmetrically to the earlier formulation, we could say that we are dealing with an *exclusion of the exclusion*, or an inclusion that implies the negation of the negation.

Third Thesis   But, in turn, this examination of the dynamic relationship between inclusion and exclusion, one that is both conflictual and reflexive, leads us to shift our attention to the most concretely political aspect of this dilemma, which will involve the entrance onto the scene of *subjects* and relationships between subjects. Variations in inclusion and exclusion are not impersonal processes: they are relationships of force exercised by institutions and power apparatuses over individual and collective subjects. The question that they imply never simply takes the form of *who is excluded from what* (from what ability to belong, from which rights)? But always also the form: *who excludes (from what, from where)?*

Here, evidently, the experiences of racial segregation and sexism are paradigm cases. If the political community functions like a "club" to which one can be either admitted or refused access, we must ask how it is that the "rightful members" were admitted, how they decided on the rules for admission, and how their active participation translates into preserving the rules. In other words, there is good reason to write the political history of a community of citizens around the moments when it has been open or closed. The practical implications of this are obvious. There could be no exclusion of women from full citizenship (implying the exercise of political and professional responsibilities), or from certain civil rights, without the constitution of a citizenship that functioned (and continues to function) as a "men's club," in which individuals (male or not) continually endeavored to enforce these rules, by inscribing equaliberty within an internal border that was presented as "natural," "traditional," or "socially necessary." We can make the same observation, all else being equal, with regard to the phenomena of racial and cultural discrimination, which erect barriers (sometimes symbolic, sometimes material) that deny certain human beings access to citizenship, or to its full rights, and which shape the political institution of every country in the world, liberal democracies being no exception.

What all this means is that *it is the community itself that excludes*, not only in the form of bureaucratic rules and procedures, but also in the form of a consensus of its members, which is itself more or less politically "motivated." To put it in clear terms, we would say that *it is always citizens*, "knowing" and "imagining" themselves as such, *who exclude from citizenship* and who, thus, "produce" *non-citizens in such a way as to make it possible for them to represent their own citizenship to themselves as a "common" belonging*. We must nonetheless offer two qualifications, perhaps even mitigations, alongside this radical conclusion, which implies that citizenship as exclusion of the exclusion must always be grounded upon struggle. First, the degree to which the citizens of a community participate in the exclusion of non-citizens is never uniform: it involves degrees and exceptions, protests and transgressions of consensus. Second, the participation of some in the exclusion of others is rarely *direct*, but for the most part *indirect, delegated* in a certain sense to the institutions of citizenship that "represent" the citizens or stem from their authorization – which also means that the management of exclusions constitutes an *implicit clause* in the representation and delegation of power. As we know, in the democratic institution of citizenship, it is more often than not up to the *law* to provide a transcendental sanction for all manner of social categorizations and administrative procedures, or to transform cultural, ideological, and sociological distinctions into universal, "normative," rules.

Here we arrive at another aspect of the "conflictuality" embedded in the unstable equilibrium of the processes of inclusion and exclusion, insofar as they bring into play relationships of society, state, and law. Because the participation of citizens in the exclusion of non-citizens passes through the delegation of power to the state, the line of demarcation between these two types of humans is sanctified or sacralized. But owing to the fact that the state and the law responsible for carrying out this differentiation are themselves fragile authorities whose legitimacy can be contested and whose sovereignty is at times shaky, the exclusionary rule is constantly exposed to perverse uses. We see this especially in contemporary societies where racism and xenophobia are not the result of true conflicts of interest between culturally or historically foreign communities so much as mechanisms for projecting the social anxieties of the majority. What the nationals of a given country are more or less explicitly "requesting," for example, when they demand stronger exclusionary measures targeting immigrants, or what the French far right calls "priority for nationals," is an a priori guarantee against discrimination or the degradation of social status, which they are afraid they might be next in line for, especially if they happen to be poor or socially disadvantaged. Naturally, there are enormous differences of degree between these phenomena, which are never automatic. Yet they are regular enough, being periodically reactivated in the context of "crises," for us to see the signs of a worrisome affinity between "populism" and democratic citizenship itself. The *gray area* discussed earlier thus appears not only as a zone of indecision between inclusion and exclusion, but as a zone in which exclusion is indirectly demanded of the "representative" state by a quasi-community of quasi-citizens, or by citizens uncertain of their rights and their recognition.

The Concept of the Political and the Anthropology of Citizenship

The discussion above is doubtless a simplification of the complete historical account of relationships of citizenship and exclusion. Nevertheless, we can hope that these discussions can initiate a shift in our manner of understanding the "concept of the political," for which Schmitt's famous definition given in his 1932 *The Concept of the Political* would represent both an obligatory reference point and a negative model (Schmitt, 1976 [1932]). It is not a question of generalizing or updating the idea that the "distinction between friend and enemy" defines what is specific to the political as opposed to the other spheres of human activity, but rather of explaining why, in a given set of circumstances, this distinction can come to express the totality of measures that join community and exclusion together, while at the same time showing itself unable to take into consideration the whole system of differences that these encompass. In order to make these two points clearer, I will describe what constitutes the quintessential paradox of *political anthropology* that is specifically associated with the development of modern national citizenship.

1   Why is it that modern citizenship, recast around universalist principles, not only has *failed* to put an end to all forms

of interior exclusion, but also has had a tendency to create new ones, granting them justifications that are themselves universal, or transcendental? The principle of equaliberty posits that, within the limits of her own community or of her politically constituted "people," every individual is the equal of, if not similar to, any other, and that no one can exercise an arbitrary, discretionary, authority over another. But the history of civil codes and bourgeois constitutions is one of discriminations founded not only upon "common utility" (in accordance with the statement in the 1789 Declaration of the Rights of Man and Citizen, Article One: "Men are born and remain free and equal in rights. Social distinctions may be founded only upon the general good"), but also upon marginalization within humanity itself. The retreat of statutory *inequality*, whether traditional or conventional, would therefore have been purchased at the price of an exclusion that was even more radical, because it legitimated itself within the very idea of universality itself.

2   We must therefore assume that the extension of the principle of the rights of the citizen to "everything with a human face" (Fichte, 1973 [1795]) and their foundation upon the "rights of man," which represents not so much a natural origin as a transcendental guarantee of access to citizenship, constitute not only a justification for the elimination of discrimination (or a *struggle* with the aim of eliminating it), but also a reason behind the renewal of these discriminations and of their extension beyond previous limits, albeit under a new form. Once individuals and groups can no longer be excluded from citizenship on the basis of status or social background, they must be excluded precisely *as* "*humans*," as types of humans that are different from the rest. And what is striking is that this mechanism of exclusion that is itself universalist does not disappear as the "foundational" discourse of natural rights gives way to a purely legalistic

constitutionalism, in which government practices find their foundations in law or science (or, more often than not, a combination of the two). On the contrary, this discrimination becomes diversified and coextensive with society, within the framework of what Foucault called "biopolitics." The only explanation for this is that there is a necessary structural co-occurrence between the mode through which modern political "universalist" communities (primarily the *nation*) are constituted and the transformation of general *anthropological differences* (differences of gender, differences of age, differences between the normal and the pathological, etc.) into principles of exclusion, which has granted modern "humanism" its intensely contradictory content.

This is what Foucault demonstrated in a series of works, the analytical precision of which can (and must) be debated, but whose main point represents an irreversible epistemological break: the transcendental universality of the species and the discriminating and discriminatory functions of anthropological differences are not incompatible; they form two faces of the same discourse, one that began with the philosophy and politics of the Enlightenment (as we already saw with the construction of Kantian *anthropology* (Kant, 2006 [1798]). But Foucault (2003a) also demonstrated, particularly with the example of "abnormality," that this necessary co-occurrence is always problematic: not only because the universalism of "the rights of man" allows for recourse to an *ideal* that can be seized upon by any of the categories victimized by exclusion, but also because the line drawn by exclusion is intrinsically unstable and ultimately elusive. This is why the category of "abnormal" constantly oscillates between psychiatric references and criminological ones, such that the marginalization of "abnormals" is contested between the medical and legal apparatuses. Here it might be useful to draw a comparison with Arendt's (1951) analyses of the contradictory relationship that existed in the nineteenth and twentieth centuries between the *closed character* of citizenship instituted within *national frameworks* and *the universalism* of access to the rights proclaimed by the nation-state (with the notable exception of its imperial and colonial extensions, where there were no citizens, but rather "subjects," or "subject races").

Thus the extreme and yet revelatory position of *racist states* such as Nazi Germany or apartheid South Africa in the history of modern states, because they tended (locally, provisionally, but with dramatic exterminatory consequences) to focus on this contradiction in one of its terms alone, by developing radical plans for the purification or segregation of the species. We know that eugenics programs (the forced sterilization of "undesirables," for example) were implemented throughout the twentieth century, in the Nordic social democracies as in many US states (including California). As the Frankfurt School theorists (Horkheimer and Adorno, 1972 [1944]), as well as critics of modernity such as Zygmunt Bauman (1999), pointed out, this nihilistic and radically anti-humanist tendency was not external to modern humanism; rather, it formed its other face (or its other stage), which was "normally" more or less repressed. Underneath the *political* sphere there is always also an *un-political* sphere (Esposito, 1993).

This leads us to suggest that there can be a gradual intermingling of models of exclusion that justify themselves in idealist terms, appealing to a definition of man in which he is predestined for citizenship, and those that justify themselves in materialist or positivist terms, identifying psychological or physiological characteristics that would mark the "inferior" capacities of certain humans (depending on the era, women, manual laborers, abnormals, foreigners, and colonial populations or immigrants). In the contemporary situation, in which the classical representation of national citizenship is subject to violent tensions, certain situations of exclusion can illustrate the model of Agamben's (2005) "normalized state of exception," which is grounded in Schmitt,

but others simply reflect the quasi-transcendental impossibility of *representing the community* (or "the common"),
whether in terms of interests or in terms of rights and reciprocal obligations (Nancy, 1990).

The whole question rests in knowing whether the collective
"actors" of globalization, whom we could describe as the
"citizens to come" of the cosmopolitan space, will as a majority search for a transnational model for "governing" discriminations and exclusions, or, on the contrary, for a new
universalism that would be as "egalitarian" as possible. This
is why concrete questions such as the rights to movement and
residence (going beyond the individual "hospitality" that
Kant made into the principal content of cosmopolitanism)
have had a determinative impact on the evolution of the very
idea of "citizen" itself. Or maybe these fundamentally transnational rights will be recognized not only as "rights of man"
(which already happened, with a few qualifications, in the
1948 Universal Declaration of Human Rights), but as the
elements of political citizenship. Or perhaps post-national
"governance" will translate into the increased relegation and
repression of "nomadic" and "diasporic" populations. This
would mean that the sovereignty of states would be concen-
trated specifically in their policing-oriented roles, such as
regulating borders and the movements of populations, potentially leaving it up to the international bodies and NGOs to
take care of the enormous "humanitarian" problem represented by the growing mass of "non-citizens" who are, as
such, *from neither here nor there.* We would therefore end up
with a particularly violent, and probably unstable, transformation of intensive universality into extensive universality,
creating a "post-national citizenship" based upon communication networks and globalized trade (as Saskia Sassen
[2006], in particular, has proposed), but at the price of a
symmetrical generalization of the rule of exclusion.

6

The Aporia of Conflictual
Democracy

Once we have put back into question the idea of a citizenship founded on consensus, or in search of a higher form of community consensus, we must then shift to examining the relationship between democracy and struggle or conflict. It may very well be that the idea of "conflictual democracy" remains unavoidably aporetic, at least so long as we examine it from the institutional perspective alone. But it is this very aspect that would make possible a critical examination of the role of institutions in politics.

The main body of thought and discussion surrounding this question comes from the recent era, beginning with J.G.A. Pocock's landmark work (Pocock, 1975), which offered a rereading of Machiavelli's analyses, found in his *Discourses on Livy* (1996 [1531]), of how the republican form was reinforced through a process of developing and representing social conflict within the Roman institutions of the republican period. After a series of revolts against the patricians and established order, the "poor" or the "lower orders" were granted their own representation within the state, which allowed them to more or less completely block policies that went against their interests. Around this model of a "Tribune of the Plebs," a new type of material constitution emerged, one that was no longer comparable to the "mixed constitution" of the ancient theorists. It was even, in a sense, the exact opposite. In an effort to interpret the type of state that established itself in the mid-twentieth century in European countries (particularly France and Italy), in which social citizenship was imposed by pressure from communist parties that were officially revolutionary but in practice fought for reforms, the French political scientist Georges Lavau (1981) specifically described these parties as playing the "tribunal role" (*fonction tribunicienne*), an expression that has since become standard in political science. The exercise of modern tribunal power has ultimately contributed to the stabilization of the nation-state, but it has done so through a specific manner of organizing the class struggle. We should not be too hasty to describe this as a betrayal or double-dealing. Instead, we should analyze it as a characteristic example of the "unintended consequences" of political practice. Without the utopian revolutionary perspective (or its partial equivalent in social democratic countries, which we might call the "spirit of scission"), class struggles are neither sizable nor durable enough to force the bourgeoisie to compromise, and especially not to make public sphere a site of a true conflict. Compromise, which will be more or less advantageous to one of the parties, is a chance result, not a deliberate objective. It does not presume the convergence of interests.

In fact, political philosophy would periodically rediscover this Machiavellian idea, at times to describe the essence of *phases of transition*, or instability between regimes and heterogeneous "dominations," at times in an attempt to understand what it is about *"democracy" that makes it a "regime" unlike others*, from the perspective of its critics and its defenders alike. This idea therefore brings together some of the deepest dilemmas inherent in the idea of a "constitution of citizenship" or a "republican form" of the political.

Violence and Counter-Violence

It is useful to mention here that, in keeping with the previous chapter, there is a complex relationship between the idea of *exclusion* and that of *conflict*. Many forms of exclusion can immediately spark conflict, or have the potential to do so, to the extent that they give rise to resistance, demands for equality, and repressive policies. On the other hand, exclusion from the political sphere, where the legitimacy of collective action is decided, can be a very effective means of neutralizing conflict, or of suppressing the forms of it that put into question the distribution and use of power. It can, at least provisionally (although this provisional moment can last for quite a long time), render powerless those who would defy power-holders. This is especially conspicuous when the procedures of segregation or apartheid, of disqualification and surveillance, come together, whether it be at the national, imperial, or transnational level, to limit political participation to the members of an "elite" or of a "dominant community." This is what anthropologist Philomena Essed (2005) has called a "preference for sameness." It is often tied to nationalism and postcolonial racism, and in practice it often functions in a similar manner. It is never solely a question of marginalizing individual "cases" or "subjects" from political participation, but of exercising a *preventative counter-violence*, and therefore of prohibiting social (or "cultural") violence from attaining a political form in the proper sense by keeping it at the level of what Gramsci (1992) called the "corporative" modality.

At this point, several questions emerge that are as difficult as they are important, specifically:

1   There is the question of how the relationship between *conflict and violence* is established, theoretically but also historically. Not only is the preventative repression of conflict generally extremely violent, which is to say, it implies

the dissymmetrical use of all the instruments (police, law, ideology) of institutional power, but it also involves a (riskier) *manipulation of the violence* that cannot always be entirely kept at bay, and which upon emerging exposes itself to "legitimate" punishment (as we saw in most of the recent cases of urban violence).

2   Then we have the question of how exclusion can be conceptualized and organized in a *space without borders,* one without an exterior, or, better yet, one that would be *pure exteriority,* as is the case with the global space in the era of market globalization, in which states have increasingly tended to operate in the service of market exchange and financial interests. Perhaps it is in precisely these conditions that *internal exclusion* will transform itself once again into the production of "disposable humans" (*hommes jetables*) (Ogilvie, 2012) or "non-persons" (Dal Lago 2009) who are permanently exposed to elimination of one form or another. In any event, whether the violence of excluded groups is manipulated or the groups themselves are eliminated through a process of depersonalization, it is the possibility itself of political *action* that is neutralized or destroyed, by being demoted from the collective to the individual level. This is why such situations represent an extreme limit for democracy, but also, by their contrast, illustrate that the essence of democracy is the maximization of the capacity of its citizens for political action. "Active citizenship" is the tautological expression used to designate this capacity.

Against the backdrop of this negative condition of possibility, we can then examine the three aporias inherent in the idea of conflictual democracy: (1) the aporia of the relationship between *conflict and institutional legitimacy;* (2) the aporia of the *different types of political conflicts* that have the potential to play a "constituent" role, depending on whether they display symmetrical or dissymmetrical relationships of power and interests; and (3) the aporia of the historical forms for regulating or neutralizing conflict, and of the relationship of these to the antithetical forms of "voluntary servitude" and "civil disobedience."

Liberalism, Pluralism, and the Representation of Conflict

Even if our examination of this issue will have to remain incomplete, we should begin by returning to the principal question underlying the aporia of an institutionalization of conflict. This question contains the key as to why democracy – if it is indeed a regime in the proper sense of the term – always seems in a sense to be an "impossible" regime, but also, paradoxically, an indestructible one. We could certainly posit that democracy, in general, is a "regime" that *renders conflict legitimate*, albeit under quite different justifications and to varying degrees. It all depends, of course, on the forms, causes, and modalities of conflict, as well as the means that can be employed to limit or suspend it. It is therefore tempting to say that if democracy can *become* a political regime, it would be able to do so insofar as it could manage to legitimate conflict within certain limits, in such a manner as to avoid resulting in community self-destruction, in the paradigmatic form of a real or metaphorical "civil war." Here, the antithesis of the *polis* and of *stasis* reappears as a model continuously repeating itself (Loraux, 2006).

But, in turn, the way in which this proposition comes to be realized is susceptible to a high degree of variation, the theoretical importance of which should not be overlooked. These variations are relevant not only to the scope of the possibilities for conflict, but also especially to the *finality* of its regulation, whether the goal is to promote its expression as a constituent reality of democratic existence, or, on the contrary, to stifle it as much as is necessary for a *rule* (particularly a rule of law) to be imposed and an authority manifested. In other words, democracy comes to seem like an institutional machine that *transforms conflicts* without ever purely and simply abolishing them, that causes them to transition from a destructive role to a constructive one, or just from a savage form to a "civilized" or "civil" one, which could be controlled from either within or without (Machiavelli's *conflitto civile*, as opposed to "civil war") (Gaille-Nikodimov, 2004).

We should note that these two formulations do not refer to exactly the same concept. The first formulation is logically "stronger," because it evokes a conflict concerning interests or ideologies, which could be seen as *contributing* to the existence of democracy, of which it is, in the end, the properly political "moment." The second formulation, by contrast, is "weaker," because it is grounded on the negative idea that democratic rules (as opposed to authoritarian or totalitarian rules) are better adapted to the "moderation" of social struggles over the long term. This could very easily represent a logical and political *circle*: if it turned out to be the case, for example, that "democratic struggles" are precisely those that lend themselves to institutional moderation, which is to say, those struggles that have always already neutralized their own "excesses." Here, of course, it becomes crucial to distinguish between different types of conflict (as did historians and sociologists such as Charles Tilly and Ralf Dahrendorf, as well as philosophers such as Chantal Mouffe, and, of course, we cannot leave out Simmel's groundbreaking analyses), not only because some can be more violent in nature, but also because of the types of collective "forces" and "actors" that these conflicts introduce into politics.

At this point it is necessary to point out that such a conception – either "weak" or "strong" – of conflict is in no way alien to the *liberal tradition*. On the contrary, the liberal tradition includes a great number of interpretations of this idea. As a political doctrine (as Raymond Aron, in particular, emphasized in 1965), liberalism is characterized by its insistence on the importance of *pluralism* in politics. Moreover, in order for pluralism not to be an empty idea, devoid of reality, we cannot think about it independently of a certain degree of antagonism or, better yet, of *agonism*, whether in the form of competition between rival ideologies, or conflict among social interests. This principle should not be conflated with the principle of representation, but they are not mutually exclusive, either. Historically, an insistence on pluralism was linked to an insistence by advocates of liberalism on the necessity of putting an end to such antithetical forms as despotism (even when "enlightened"), absolutism, and totalitarianism, doing so in reality or in the imagination – perhaps even in myth. We can therefore understand why this insistence oscillates between an "optimistic" view, according to which pluralism contains a positive value, or an expansive virtue, which turns conflict (particularly the conflict of opinions) into a means of creating of political liberty, and a "pessimistic" view, according to which pluralism must be constantly protected from dangers that threaten it both internally and externally, which is basically Popper's view (Popper, 1945). Here it would be fundamentally important to demonstrate how the liberal political discourse, from Spinoza all the way to Rawls and Habermas, was always in a certain sense *restricting* the scope and field of conflicts that could potentially enter into the "game" of pluralism and its specific agonism – before it would be opened in a much more uncertain way by the irruption of questions of "multiculturalism" (Kymlicka, 1995; Leggewie, 1990).

In his 1672 *Tractatus Theologico-Politicus*, Spinoza (2007 [1672]) proposed a democratic strategy founded on the premise that all religious convictions could be seen as ways for individuals to incline themselves to "obedience," which is to say, the recognition of the primacy of common interests, as expressed by the republic, over individual or private "ambitions." This is certainly an example of a limiting rule, but one that makes no prescriptions relating to the nature of the ideologies in conflict against one another, or of the interests that these ideologies express (which marks a clear difference between Spinoza's view and the idea of tolerance that Locke was defending at the time). With Rawls (1993) came the idea that a community of citizens presupposes an "overlapping consensus," which establishes rules for moderating the conflicts that arise from oppositions between "substantive conceptions" of the *good*. These conceptions are currents of thought, either secular or religious, that are not satisfied with attempting to define the good or virtue using formal criteria, such as the Kantian "ability to transform an individual maxim into a universal law of humanity," but wish to provide these ideas with determined *content*, specifically a "good" or "just" *way of life*. For Rawls, this consensus is the moral equivalent of a certain idea of rationality, or of justice as the establishment of a collective rationality – which in turn would need to be guaranteed and reproduced, a role that would be played by laws and especially by education. Lastly, with Habermas (1984), we find a description of pluralism that has normative value. For him, a necessary precondition of pluralism is that the "parties" of a social and ideological conflict all consent to abide by the rules of *public debate*, because it is argumentation in the public space that allows for the transition from an *irreducible* antagonism – which leads to the disqualification of one of the positions involved (and potentially the elimination of those who defended this position) – to a regime of debate and communication, whose ethical ideal is the agreement of all citizens on the legitimacy of a given policy (perhaps at the cost of compromises made by a given party).

With Rawls as with Habermas, and perhaps even already with Spinoza – all of whom were rationalists, despite the distance separating their different conceptions of "reason" – we find the implicit premise that consensus (or at least the continuing *possibility* of consensus) must in the end either prevail over the expression of contradiction or *transform*, "overcome," this expression. This explains a typical expression of Spinoza's in the *Tractatus Politicus* (2005 [1677]: III, § 2): in a free republic, power ultimately rests with a "free multitude" who act "as if they were led by a single soul." The "as if" (*veluti*) is clearly fundamental; it is what marks the distance between a conflict-less "unanimity" that is created or imagined, and a "community" that results from the regulation of conflict "under the direction of reason." But the result of this is the continual return of an aporia specific to liberalism: at the critical juncture, when conflict exceeds its purely symbolic forms of expression – conventions of collective "debate," existing institutional channels for the representation of contradictory interests – and therefore the possibility of government and obedience, political "rationality" is no longer tenable, and there is a return to the alternative of either neutralizing conflict or repressing it. A conflict that threatens the constitutional order, as flexible or open as it might wish itself to be, is no longer playing by the pluralistic "rules of the game," and is therefore incompatible with liberalism. This contradiction is independent of the question of whether the origin of this conflict lies in class relationships, religious antagonisms, "cultural" and "racial" differences, or an overdetermined conjunction of these factors, as is generally the case. But, inversely, can we truly say that a conflict that is "channeled" by means of rules that force it to contribute to a consensus, or to "translate" itself into an exchange of arguments, is still a *real* conflict, and not a legal *fiction*? Does not a *limited*, or even *self-limited*, conflict pre-emptively exclude anything that, in a given society, carries true political stakes: liberation struggles, emancipatory demands,

revolts against injustice or inequality, and thus any historically significant transformations?

Such an argument must be more precise, however, given
that it seems to neglect the difference between the "social"
and the "political." And, in the modern era, this difference
is always embedded in the various models for the institutionalization of conflict. Liberalism, which from this point of
view appears as an extreme form, suggests that the elements
of conflictuality – when it involves *interests* or especially
opinions – come from "civil society." In other words, these
elements are rooted in the *social activities of individuals*,
and they must be "expressed" or "represented" in the
language and forms of "political society" in order for their
resolution to be authorized, in other words, for initially
incompatible tendencies to be rendered compatible. The principal function of the state would specifically be to oversee
this transformation. But, in turn, one might offer the objec-
tion that the collective "actors" engaged in a given conflict
can only become historically decisive once they have mini-
mized the distance between their social interests and their
political objectives (or once they have found a *direct* political
expression of their social interests), and no longer take it
for granted that the existing state will play the role of
arbiter between antagonistic opinions or social interests.
Once antagonism has "politicized the social" and, inversely,
as is clearly the case with the class struggle, the state stops
being impartial, it then emerges as an *interested party* to the
conflict, taking sides or at least becoming predisposed
towards certain solutions rather than others (precisely those
that preserve its form, its institutions). It therefore becomes
a part of the power struggle. Clearly, historical actors are
those who *change* the relationship of the social to the political, forcing needs and interests to be recognized not only as
"particular interests," but as *general interests of society as
a whole*, which would be potentially universalizable, thus

transforming the procedures for the establishment of consensus, the criteria of political rationality, and the very function of the state itself. A good example of this is the emergence of social citizenship after a long historical period of class struggle and confrontation between the labor movement and the "bourgeois" (or even "liberal") state. A conflict that could truly be called "real" or "effective" is never satisfied with respecting the established rules, because its stakes are precisely the constitution and even the content itself of pluralism.

Democracy as "Illegitimate Domination" and "Agonistic Pluralism"

If this were true, then we would have to admit that any effective political conflict involves an element of *illegitimacy*. And if democracy and conflict maintain a constituent relationship, we would then have to say that democracy is, in a very delimited sense, a "regime of illegitimate power" (which is another way of saying that it is not a "regime" in the same sense as others). This was precisely the hypothesis that Max Weber outlined in different passages from his unfinished posthumously published work *Economy and Society* (which is in fact a general treatise on anthropology and political theory).

Weber (1978 [1922]) gave a formal definition of the "legitimacy" (*Geltung*) of any form of domination or power as the *probability* (*Chance*) *that it would be obeyed*, its "commandments" executed, its "authority" respected (which goes especially for the authority of the *law*). This definition is already essentially conflictual or agonistic, given that it suggests that legitimacy is the result of an unstable equilibrium between tendencies to obey and tendencies to disobey (or, if we consider its extension, that it involves a determined proportion of "cases" of obeying or "disobeying"). For the word "legitimacy" to have any meaning, it must certainly be that the former are prevalent (or "normal") and the latter residual (or "exceptional"). But what is specific to a relationship of this kind is that in certain circumstances it can be reversed, and the exception can become the rule. This is why this kind of definition falls into the "realist" or "pragmatic" tradition, which also includes thinkers like Spinoza (whose other side we discover here, in which obedience is the pragmatic objective of a state that is *indifferent to the motives* that give rise to this obedience among subjects, which is also, we should note, a way of widening the scope of freedom of conscience), and Foucault, for whom all "power" is in an unstable relationship with "counter-powers" or "resistances," which it uses to reinforce itself, but which can also, in certain circumstances, prevail over it and give rise to a new institutional form.

But this is not all, because for Weber – as we know – this formal definition was embedded in a historical typology of forms of domination that was also a problematic of the modernization of political societies. Here we should pay special attention to the importance of the type that he calls "bureaucratic." We should do so not only because he associates it with the development of the law and the capitalist economy (which generalizes the "rational cost–benefit calculation" of individual and collective action), but because it typically presupposes the "ignorance of the people," who – more often than not unknowingly – delegate their ability to assess reality to experts (even if it sometimes means rebelling against the consequences of these expert decisions when the opportunity presents itself). Even when, as we mentioned above, this break is compensated for by educational systems and the "meritocratic" recruitment of experts, or by the *public nature* of their deliberations (which is rarely total in our bourgeois democracies and which is increasingly diminishing within the context of globalized "governance"), there necessarily remains a contradictory element between the "egalitarianism" implicit in the idea of democracy, and the "oligarchic" nature of expertise. This allows us to understand both how citizens "normally" submit themselves to the state bureaucracy, and how, in situations of crisis, of popular mistrust and the delegitimization of the established powers, citizens recreate conflict by "irrationally" rejecting expertise that claims to incarnate rationality.

Above all, we should supplement the above ideas with a – partly historical, partly allegorical – description of democracy as an "illegitimate domination" by the people (or by the multitude of the people), which Weber (1957 [1921]) proposed in his interpretation of the history of *citystates*, spanning from the ancient cities of Greece and Rome up to the Italian cities of the Middle Ages and Renaissance. This description is implicitly grounded on Machiavelli's interpretation, in *Discourses on Livy* (1996 [1531]), of the place and actions of the "plebs" or the "*popolo minuto.*" For him, they were both a real threat to the monopoly of power in the hands of oligarchs or "patricians" (a threat that would at times express itself in real insurrections) and a positive construction of a "counter-power" that was an obstacle to the tyranny of a minority. For Machiavelli, the little people were not looking to exercise power themselves; they only wished "not to be dominated" or oppressed. From Weber's perspective, this history provides an inverse illustration of the implications of his concept of legitimacy: domination that, as such, cannot exclude disobedience (or whose laws are as likely to be obeyed as to be defied, argued, transformed) is "illegitimate" by definition. This comes down to the perilous introduction of an element of "anarchic" citizenship into the very idea of democracy, one that would be a necessary precondition for the establishment of democracy. Such an element is evidently what liberal constitutionalism always tries to either exclude or ignore: the periodic or permanent, open or latent, manifestation of a conflictuality that cannot be reduced to the rules of representation or communication, that remains *excessive* in relation to any consensus, or that pushes agonism beyond the limits of a "coherent" pluralism. But this excess that cannot be controlled a priori would also be a necessary precondition for the institution of democracy, because it would permit *real* conflicts to enter into the cycle of the legitimation and delegitimation of power. This is a remarkably realist, but also very ambiguous, formulation. For Weber, whose political anthropology was founded on the idea of a permanent struggle (or "war") between "values," this translated into both an admiration of revolutions and insurrections and a warning against the danger of destabilizing the state inherent in radical democratization, which would release antagonistic forces. We know that Weber was preoccupied here not only with ancient history, but also with the contemporary political crises of war in Europe and socialist revolutions. In this we can see the idea advanced by Chantal Mouffe (2000) that democracy is a *paradoxical form* of politics, because a pure "agonism" is in a certain sense impossible, or untenable. What Weber was desperately searching to inscribe in citizenship itself was not the *complementarity* of conflict (or struggle) and institution (or order), but rather the *immanence of each term with the other*, which would require each one to define itself by its opposite: all conflicts can be subsumed into institutions, but all institutions are potential sites of future insurrections.

Here Mouffe is drawing from Schmitt (1976) and his "concept of the political," founded on the permanent distinction between friend and enemy. But in truth, she is closer to Weber, and thus Foucault and his suggestion in *Society Must Be Defended* (Foucault, 2003b) that we must reverse Clausewitz's famous formulation ("war is the continuation of politics by other means") and see the political as the "continuation of war by other means." Schmitt's criteria are criteria for the *politicization* of human activities, which could in principle be applied to all domains (including those of religion and art). It begins with antagonism and from there establishes a boundary between "camps," such that, for each of them, *internal* solidarity and the community effect are maximized, while, *between them*, hostility and incompatibility are also maximized. Of course, such a conception of conflict (based on a comparison of class struggle and nationalism) also has institutional implications. It postulates that the function of the state is to *internalize all solidarities* (in the privileged form of a "homogeneous people," which fascism went so far as to attempt to "create") and to *externalize all forms of hostility*. This implies first subordinating all conflict to the imperative of national unity, and then establishing, each time it becomes necessary, a "state of exception" through which "internal enemies" can be identified and eliminated, or at least forcibly returned to unanimity. Schmitt's criteria therefore begin by affirming a primacy or autonomy of the political that places conflict above the state and its separate power. But this immediately reverses itself into its opposite, making the state into the sovereign actor in charge of distributing "war" or hostility between its two correlative theaters: internal war and external war. There is no sign of pluralism as such in this reversal, which can be extended infinitely if it turns out that the border between the internal and the external cannot be defined once and for all. Mouffe wanted to avoid this conclusion, and this is why she tried to find a "tempered" use for Schmitt, in which the idea of agonism would serve as a corrective to the liberal view of politics as the realm of argumentation and the legal norm without any true *political alternative*, all while distancing itself from "the moment of sovereign decision" when the state *appropriates conflict*, in order to direct its outcome in the direction of a certain conservative or counter-revolutionary political "order."

With Foucault, things are more complicated. He began in the 1970s with a purely "agonistic" representation, applying the idea of politics as war in another form to all manner of spheres of power (or of "power-knowledge"), which were all similarly structured by the confrontation of power and resistance, legality and illegality, instances of authority and transgression, and which did not refer back to any ultimate "arbiter of power." But it was probably not by accident that he subsequently evolved towards a more general problematic of "governmentality," which, significantly, he saw as being exercised both at the level of the individual and at the collective level of a "social" that includes the state, but which can never be absorbed by the state's monopoly of power. In this later view, there no longer seems to be any room for "pure" conflictuality. This also corresponds to the idea that we can only identify an element of conflict that is constituent of the political *indirectly*. It is through the analysis of the transformation of power relationships by the resistances that they bring into being, and which are necessary for the very constitution of these relationships, that we can identify what Foucault (1975) was inspired to call "the noise of the battle." This is what doubtless underlies his position: conflict is irreducible, but it is never "pure" or "absolute," outside of all rules and any "game." It does not even remain within the limits of an *agon*. This is why subjects and societies alike oscillate between moments of pluralism, or the *recognition of differences*, and moments of *normalization*, which impose homogeneous, constricting, models.

Institution and Conflict as a Dissymmetrical Relationship

Our discussion has not allowed us to emerge out of this aporia. But it does have the following important philosophical implication: we have not discovered any miraculous possibility for identifying institution and conflict with one another, or of bringing one of them out from under the scope of the other without effectively depriving it of its content. We must therefore stick with the idea of a "conflictual democracy," which is like a horizon that continually retreats into the distance with regard to its own determination. But this also entails a couple of positive lessons:

1   The politico-metaphysical scheme of "subsuming" *a question under a political form* (which Machiavelli employed) does not work. The only workable framework is that of a *unity of opposites*, or of a chance equilibrium, oscillating between the two abstract poles of citizenship without civil conflict and conflict without institutions (which has been, in every era, the content of messianic or apocalyptic revolutions).

2   In discussing the endless oscillation that follows from this unity of opposites, we will have to reformulate and gain a better understanding of the implications of the *polarities inherent in the concept of the political*: insurrection and constitution, constituent and constituted powers, organized and spontaneous social struggles, and so on. None of these formulations can cover the others exactly, in particular because they have emerged from distinct philosophical traditions (the revolutionary tradition, the antinomies of the construction of a state that wishes to embody "popular sovereignty," the vicissitudes of "anti-authoritarian revolts," etc.). However, this is not to say that they do not share a characteristic relationship between *possible* and *real* (or, as Hegel would say, the *effective*). In all cases, to pass from the possible to the real is also to pass from a "dispersed" citizenship to an "intensified" or "activated" citizenship, *transforming the modalities of conflict* in order to give it political form or shape it into a historical "social formation."

It is in this sense that conflict is constitutive of the political: there is no *unique* or even *typical* form of social conflictuality or of its political expression. This is why the models proposed by Machiavelli (based on the idea of the "tribunal power" of the little people or of the governed), by Hegel (based on the idea of a "struggle for recognition," which today has been turned into an entire problematic of justice), by Marx (based on the idea of the class struggle as the process by which social antagonism subverts state order), by Weber (based on the idea of an "illegitimate domination" that underlies legitimate dominations), by Foucault (based on the idea of an inherent resistance to power whose potentialities for autonomy must in every case be "governed"), and even by Schmitt (based on the idea of the repercussions of the friend–enemy distinction on the constitution of the political community itself), all offer a way of thinking about this *incessant transformation*, which blocks the political from finding a definitive form. The impossibility of the institution of conflict as the "solution" to the problem of democratic citizenship does not mean that the history of citizenship was not forged out of *the conflict of institutions*, evolving from one regulation to the next, sometimes in a progressive manner (expanding equal liberty), sometimes in a regressive one (reducing or eliminating its possibility, and therefore citizenship itself).

We can also note that all of these accounts that philosophers experimented with share the common feature that they inscribe a fundamental *dissymmetry* within the conflict in question: there is no such thing as an "equal" political conflict, especially not when it comes to the struggle for equality. We might say that symmetry, whether it is that of "adversaries" or of bodies in the political space (society, the state), carries the mortal danger of neutralizing the political and "active" citizenship itself. We can see this in the history of contemporary socialism, which began with an effort by the labor movement (and by the working class itself) to rise up from its "subaltern" position, to overcome exclusion (whether this was exclusion from elementary social rights or from political representation), and arrived at a symmetry of a struggle of "class against class," and more precisely of "bourgeois states" against "proletarian states," which became symmetrical "camps" at the international level. A fair amount of the interest given to Machiavelli by contemporary theoreticians of "radical democracy" relates to the conceptual and symbolic tools that he provides for imagining "democratic transformation" in which symmetry would be indefinitely deferred.

I will now turn to the renewed difficulty that citizenship faces today in trying to keep this dialectic of institution and conflict open. My approach to this question will begin with a discussion of Wendy Brown's thesis that neo-liberalism is currently carrying out a "de-democratization."

7

Neo-Liberalism and De-Democratization

Let us begin with Brown's (2003) thesis: there is an essential difference between liberalism and neo-liberalism. The relative autonomy of the economic and political spheres, inviolable in classical liberal theory because it was the foundation of the idea of the relative externality of the state – as "night watchman" or "policeman" – with respect to the economy, has now clearly been rendered obsolete. As a result, it has become possible to combine market deregulation with permanent interventions by the state or other "agencies" of power in the field of civil society and even the private lives of subjects. These interventions "create" a new citizen out of whole cloth, one who is governed solely by the logic of economic rationality. The state disengages itself from production, the maintenance of infrastructure, social services, even scientific research, but becomes engaged more than ever in an "anthroponomy" that normalizes society, employing towards this end a whole series of "civil society" organizations as intermediaries.

A Discussion with Wendy Brown

Brown offers a tableau of how a combination of libertarian discourses with moralizing agendas and the submission of private life to religious control were implemented more or less heavy-handedly after the Reagan–Thatcher "revolution" in the West. This section of her analysis seems quite convincing. It can be complemented by other critiques of the neo-liberal paradigm, which have come from very diverse viewpoints, and all of which are based around examining how the criteria of "profitability" have been extended to private and even public activities that, in the classic capitalist model and a fortiori in the *social-national state*, were supposed to fall outside the purview of economic calculation. This would include education, scientific research, the quality of public services and administrative performance, the general level of health and security, the legal system – the list could go on.

But agreeing on this description is not enough. We must also examine the philosophical argument that accompanies it. Neo-liberalism, so the argument goes, is not just an ideology; it is a shift in the very nature of *the political* itself, one being carried out by actors at every level of society. It would represent the birth of a highly paradoxical form of political activity, as it not only neutralizes as completely as possible the element of conflictuality that was essential to classical liberalism, but also wishes to deprive it *pre-emptively* of any meaning and create a societal context in which the actions of individuals and groups (even when these actions are *violent*) fall under the jurisdiction of a single criterion: quantifiable utility. It is therefore not a question of the political but of the *anti-political*, of the preventative neutralization or abolition of sociopolitical antagonism. In an effort to account for this, Brown, influenced by Thomas Lemke (2001), suggested that we extend the category of *governmentality*, in the way that Foucault used it in his "genealogy of power" in the modern era, and take it to its furthest conclusion:

This mode of governmentality [...] convenes a "free" subject who rationally deliberates about alternative courses of action, makes choices, and bears responsibility for the consequences of these choices. In this way, Lemke argues, "the state leads and controls subjects without being responsible for them"; as individual "entrepreneurs" in every aspect of life, subjects become wholly responsible for their well-being and citizenship is reduced to success in this entrepreneurship. Neo-liberal subjects are controlled *through* their freedom – not simply [...] because freedom within an order of domination can be an instrument of that domination – but because of neo-liberalism's *moralization* of the consequences of this freedom. This means that the withdrawal of the state from certain domains and the privatization of certain state functions does not amount to a dismantling of government but, rather, constitutes a technique of governing, indeed the signature technique of neo-liberal governance in which rational economic action suffused throughout society replaces express state rule or provision. Neo-liberalism shifts "the regulatory competence of the state on to 'responsible,' 'rational' individuals [with the aim of] encourag[ing] individuals to give their lives a specific entrepreneurial form" [Lemke, 2001: 202]. (Brown, 2003: 43–4)

Let us quickly say what "governmentality" in the Foucauldian sense means: it is the whole ensemble of practices through which the "spontaneous" behavior of individuals can be modified, which boils down to the exercise of power over their own power for resistance and action, either through the establishment of "discipline" (which is inevitably as constraining as it is productive), or through the dissemination of models of ethical, and therefore cultural, behavior. Why, then, would we posit that in this respect neo-liberalism defies "traditional" definitions of the political? What would justify the idea that it transcends both "class politics" and "liberalism," a process that Brown describes as *de-democratization*, and which would also supposedly represent a mortal threat to the classical republican idea of "active citizenship"? The answer would seem to be that neo-liberalism has not been satisfied with agitating for a *retreat of the political*, but has set about *redefining* both its "subjective" side and its "objective" side. Owing to the fact that the necessary preconditions of collective *political experience*, as well as the economic constraints that are weighing on a growing number of individuals of all social classes and the value systems or conceptions of "good" and "evil" against which individuals judge their own actions, have all been affected simultaneously, Brown can talk about a *new rationality* in the philosophical sense of the term.

A generalization of this kind will, however, be problematic in several ways.

First, we should pause over the *diagnosis of the crisis* affecting traditional political systems, both liberal and authoritarian. Brown's description implies that we should see this crisis as not merely a simple downturn in a cyclical process, something that we would have seen several times before, but rather as an irreversible fact after which it would no longer be possible to return to the old modalities of action. Even if we grant this point, there remain at least two ways of interpreting the figures of subjecthood that it would entail.

One hypothesis would be that neo-liberalism is a *negative symptom* of the decomposition of traditional structures of domination and resistance to domination – even if this "tradition" was itself a recent creation, the product of the "modernization" of industrial societies (Wallerstein, 1995). This decomposition does not by itself lead to any tenable form of societal life. Instead, it results in an unstable situation (one that Durkheim would call "anomic" or Schmitt would call a "state of exception"), in which the most contradictory developments become possible in an unpredictable way.

Brown herself, in line with the Foucauldian idea of the "productivity" or the "positivity" of power, favors a different interpretation. For her, it is not so much a question of *dissolution* as of *invention*, of *another historical solution* to the problem of adapting subjects to capitalism, of adjusting individual behavior to the "politics of capital." Here the hypothesis that we formulated above of a crisis of "social citizenship" as a model for configuring the political, a crisis that would stem not only from the "revenge of capitalists" or the deterioration of the power struggle between socialism and its adversaries, but also from the development of the internal contradictions of social citizenship, can take on its full significance. A hypothesis of this kind allows us to imagine political regimes that are not only *moderately democratic* (within the limits compatible with the reproduction of structures of inequality; what Boaventura da Sousa Santos refers to as "low-intensity democracies") or *anti-democratic* (on the model of dictatorships, authoritarian regimes, or historical fascism), but in fact *a-democratic*, in the sense that the values inherent in demands for universalizable rights (which we have grouped together under the name "equaliberty") no longer play any role in their functioning or their development (even as forces of resistance or contestation).

Is this the reason why the discourse of "democratic values" and of the "spread (or even the 'exporting') of democracy" has become so invasive these days? Rendered official and banal, it has lost practically all of its ability to differentiate, and has become an integral part of the decomposition of citizenship. If such a change is indeed under way, it would be appropriate to talk about entering into a "post-history," at the same time as a "post-political," which would have to be taken far more seriously than the visions of the "end of history" popularized by Francis Fukuyama (1992) when the Soviet system collapsed in Europe. These, on the contrary, were founded on the idea of a triumph of liberalism in its classical form.

But it is not clear that this discussion can be limited to this diagnosis. On the one hand, the question arises of the extent to which the interpretation of this phenomenon of *de-democratization* reflects a *particularity of American society and history*, one that would not be immediately generalizable. Brown herself mentions that her analysis is founded on the value of the United States as a paradigm case. It might be tempting to think that the example of the United States is paradigmatic *precisely because it was not* a typical case of the creation of social citizenship and the social-national state – for reasons both geopolitical (the hegemony it exercised over the capitalist world for the whole second half of the twentieth century) and cultural (going back to the origins of its "frontier" ideology, and therefore of its character as an "individualist" colonial society), despite the depth of the egalitarian tendencies that Tocqueville observed and the intensity of class struggles during the New Deal era, which we tend to forget today. The principle of the *universality of social rights*, in particular, was never fully recognized in the US. On the other hand, as Margaret Somers (2008), among others, has noted, the oscillations between phases of state "regulation" and "deregulation" have been especially abrupt in the United States. Clearly, we cannot fault Brown for not having foreseen and accounted for the 2008 financial crisis that revealed the existence of unstable elements and radical contradictions at the heart of the Reagan–Thatcher "neo-liberal" model (which had been adopted more or less completely by subsequent "third way" politics). In fact, what we have is not so much the *stabilization* of contemporary capitalism as a *permanent crisis* or "crisis as the norm." This brings us back to our *other interpretive hypothesis*: that neo-liberalism is a symptom of dissolution.

Brown's essay was published in 2003, and it therefore predates more recent work by "critical" economists on the creation of a society founded entirely on *debt*, as well as the political *reactions* provoked by the initial stages of the crisis. For the United States, Frédéric Lordon (2008) showed the link between the policy of "securitization" – dubious lending that enabled astronomical returns on financial investments – and the extensive removal of constraints on credit that allowed households without stable resources to become debtors for life. With the development of the "sovereign debt" crises in Europe, notably in Greece, this subjugation to financial risk would backfire on states, undermining their capacity to govern. This leads us to examine another difficulty inherent in critiques of the innovation of neo-liberalism as an emergence of the *anti-political*, which is that these make the idea of "de-democratization" seem properly apocalyptic.

Positive and Negative Eschatologies

What is striking here are the analogies and differences we can discern across the century and a half that separates Brown's arguments and what we might call *Marx's nightmare*. There was an "unpublished chapter" of *Capital*, one that he ultimately chose not to include in the First Book, in which it had been intended to appear, when it was published in 1867. In this chapter he outlined the idea of a "real subsumption" (or "real submission": *reale Subsumtion*) of the labor force under capital (Marx, 1992). Why did Marx decide to set this analysis aside, given that it brought a central hypothesis of his own analysis of capital as a "social relationship" to its radical conclusion? Undoubtedly he did this for reasons that were as much political as scientific; its implications were disastrous for the idea of a *proletarian politics*. To the detriment of any idea of revolutionary organization or even of a collective consciousness of the working class, he would have had to return to an alternative that he had been distancing himself from ever since his youthful arguments concerning the "decomposition of bourgeois civil-society": either the end of the political or a messianic solution that would arise from the destruction of the necessary preconditions of the political. The "real submission" that Marx envisaged in the unpublished chapter implies that capitalism is not just a system for "consuming the labor force" with the goal of maximizing productivity through the development of various "methods" for exploiting workers or extracting surplus labor. It also becomes a system for the *(re)production of the labor force itself as commodity*, molding its "qualities," rendering them "useful" and "manageable" within a determined system of production by conditioning individual "capacities," "needs," and "desires." We also know that Marcuse attempted to offer a psycho-sociological counterpart for these Marxist theses in *One-Dimensional Man* (1964), by showing that Marx's quite general prognostic had entered into daily reality, particularly in the context of American "consumer society."

Marx's vision here is indeed apocalyptic: the extinction of the political, which had been the constituent dimension of the past, would come about as the result of economic logic pushed to the extreme. Similarly, the contemporary discourse surrounding de-democratization, inspired by Foucault, sees this extinction as the result of a specific logic of power and the invention of a new cultural "rationality." It seems as if these two representations are both haunted by the question of knowing how modern societies produce *voluntary servitude* in their own way: not only – as in La Boétie's classic work (2012 [1576]) – through the effect of the fascination engendered by the "sovereign" figure of authority (the One or the Monarch), but as a "rational" or "rationalizable" effect of depersonalizing technology, of micro-powers and daily behaviors that belong equally to the "dominant" as to the "dominated" when placed under the hegemony of certain social norms. This explains the short-circuit that was subsequently established between analyses of daily life and analyses of the exception (or the state of exception).

This is why we can observe a general return to apocalyptic themes in contemporary critical theory, either inspired by a certain Marxist tradition or by completely different reference points altogether, and which range from the idea that history has now passed into the realm of ontological "simulacrum" or the "virtual," to the idea that the political, transformed into the "biopolitical," has acquired a self-destructive dimension that makes "bare life" the final result of all subjugation to power. These were the theories of Baudrillard (1994) and Agamben (2005), respectively. In one sense, Hardt and Negri, in *Empire* (2000) and then *Multitude* (2004) and *Commonwealth* (2009), represent the most interesting attempt at a *positive reversal* of these apocalyptic themes, based on an interpretation of the "virtual" as the *immateriality of work*, but at the price of an unlimited expansion of the category of the "biopolitical." The analysis of current historical-political *processes* is therefore "trapped" between two eschatologies, one nihilistic, one redemptive. We hesitate to ask for any more "analytical" lessons from Machiavelli, Marx, or Weber.

But the question of the contemporary processes of "de-democratization" gives rise to other questions that are of capital importance for the perspective we have adopted of the decomposition of the social-national state, whether we see it as having a single cause or rather as a situation of rampant crisis that is being taken advantage of by other forces. We will not contest that there is an intrinsic link between the reversal in the direction of democratic demand-making and the intensification of procedures for the *control* of individual existence, geographical mobility, opinion, and social behavior, which employ increasingly sophisticated technology and operate on a territorial or communicational basis, either national or transnational. Deleuze (1990) spoke of this subject as the emergence of a "society of control." Let us think of the techniques for the "marking" and "tagging" of individuals, which Agamben (2004), in particular, has denounced. These are in the process of expanding into a certain kind of generalized, "real time," census of Internet users (partly through the intermediary of "social networks" such as Twitter or Facebook, which sell the "profiles" of individual users to businesses and advertisers). But let us also think of the psychological classification of children according to their future "dangerousness" – in France there was even a proposal to generalize these classifications across educational institutions (although not without controversy) – as well as the new forms of diagnostic behavioral psychiatry that have been replacing individualized psychotherapy. These are even more destructive from the perspective of the threat that they pose to the "property of oneself" that constituted the foundation of the subjecthood of the classical "citizen."

From Individualism to Populism

Above all, let us not forget that there is a *positive* counterpart to the development of these procedures of control, but one which is in a sense no less incompatible with the *political* form of citizenship. This is the development of a new individualist ethos of "self-care" (*souci de soi*), which holds that individuals must moralize their own behavior by submitting it to the criteria of maximal utility or the future productivity of their individuality. It is not recognized enough, it seems to me, that Foucault in his later years developed the theme of "self-care" *ironically*, both as a final gesture breaking with the philosophical training of his youth, and as a critical perspective from which to view the contemporary proliferation of "technologies of the self." Because this has been overlooked, attempts have been made to twist his work to fit into the neo-liberal, post-political camp. At the very least, this is a battlefield between the several traditions that try to lay claim to him. Foucault was certainly not a "socialist," but this does not mean that his radical individualism fell under the auspices of rational self-interest (which is, in its own way, a type of conformism, if not collectivism, because its driving force is the "imitational" behavior of consumers and speculators).

Recognizing the dark side of this ethos brings us to what Castel, in particular, described as *negative individualism*, which he associates with the dismantling and destruction of the institutions of "social security" along with the forms of solidarity and socialization that made it possible for individuals across generations to *affiliate* with a "community of citizens." The "unaffiliated" (or *disincorporated*) individual – for example, the young proletarian with neither job nor prospect of stable employment, whether of immigrant background or not – is a subject who is permanently the target of contradictory injunctions: he must behave like an "entrepreneur of himself," according to the new code of neo-liberal values, in such a way as to display autonomy, the necessary preconditions of which have been simultaneously denied him and placed beyond his reach. Suzanne de Brunhoff (1986) has already reminded us that we have Hayek to thank for reformulating the principle of the *homo oeconomicus* into the form: each individual should behave like a small bank. Brown, for her part, borrowed from Lemke the idea of a neo-liberal rationality that encourages individuals to "give their life the form of a business." We can ask ourselves if the development of "ethical citizenship" and of "volunteerism" – which has, in Italy for example, cushioned the dismantling of social security, doing so through the traditions of charity and solidarity of Catholic and even communist organizations (Muehlebach, 2012) – will be enough to reverse these trends, especially if they are aggravated by a downturn in the economic climate and the displacement of productive activities to other regions of the world-economy.

This explains the hopelessness we see, but also the extreme violence that is directed inwardly as much as against others: the violence of *devalorization*. It also explains the search for compensatory communities, which are often founded on an imaginary image of the all-powerful collective (or, as Derrida and Roberto Esposito would say, of "autoimmunity"). Such communities are just as *negative* and *impossible* as the individualities produced by the dismantling of social citizenship, or as state communities are in the process of becoming. Ideally, such communities can be constructed around a local base, in the form of ethno-cultural or micro-territorial "gangs" (*bandes*) (Body-Gendrot, 2001). Or these groups can project themselves into the global space by "globalizing" the religious or racial (postcolonial) imagination through networks of communication that control these groups as much as they are their tools. Unless, of course, these groups are able to successfully "dialecticize" these oppositions, through revolts that are local (communicating with each other through the "web" of the internet) and spontaneous (but that also owe an inheritance to the experience of previous generations of militants).

Thus the question re-emerges of the forms and role of "populism" in the contemporary political space. Ernesto Laclau (2002) was right to argue that "populism" in general should not be stigmatized, or conflated with fascism, not only because the thing that is actually forbidden under this typically "projective" name is usually the *participation of the masses in the political*, but also because, in a sense, we must admit that there would no longer be any "people" in politics without "populism," no "nation" without "nationalism," and no "commons" without "communism." And, each time, it is the ambiguity as to what these names for collective activity *cover* that is problematic. Certain forms of populism, despite their ambiguity or perhaps because of it, seem necessary for the generalization of a political discourse that would be able to transcend (or integrate) the specific demands of different emancipatory movements, in such a way as to question a heterogeneous multiplicity of forms of domination. This was Laclau's thesis, which attempted to reformulate what Gramsci had called "hegemony." He even made populism into the very *concept itself* of political democracy. If he was right on this point, we will have to admit that the specter of populism has always haunted the dialectic of insurrection and constitution – for better or for worse. This is quite possible. And it is perhaps one of the reasons that led Rancière to distrust certain uses or consequences of his own formulation, in which democracy was defined by "demands by the share-less."

But we must also ask the inverse question, for which it would be difficult to imagine a *universally valid* answer outside of hypotheticals: in what conditions does a "populist" modality of identifying with the missing community, or the imaginary community, become (or remain) a framework for mobilization towards *democratic* objectives? What distinguishes equality (or equaliberty), even when utopian, from the argument that there is an *equivalence* between the discourses and images that different groups employ to identify with the same "power bloc"? When must we say, on the contrary, that populism as a "communal fiction" is simply the screen onto which are projected the imaginary compensations and retributions brought on by pauperization and de-socialization, the production of "negative individuals," the stigmatization and the exclusion of bearers of "alterity" or "foreignness"? But are the two branches of this alternative ever truly *separate*, such that collective political practice would no longer have to *disassociate them in practice*, by deploying a capacity for mobilization and a capacity for civilization through the means of a determined imaginary depiction of citizenship?

Crisis of Representation and "Counter-Democracy"

We cannot separate a discussion of the ambiguous effects of the conjunction between affiliation and disaffiliation, communal incorporation and internal exclusion, negative and positive individualism, from a discussion of the *crisis of representation* in contemporary political systems. This is another feature of the political transformations that we can attribute to "neo-liberalism." Thousands of pages have been published on this subject, which has perhaps become the most privileged commonplace in contemporary political science. We cannot neglect this entirely, far from it, from our perspective of a *critique of the political in the age of the "end of the political"*; it would be too hasty, and reductive, as it is in a certain Marxist (or Rousseauian) dogma, to conflate the question of representation in general with that of *parliamentarianism*, which only represents one of its aspects and one of its possible historical forms.

It was in its role as guarantor of pluralist political systems that parliamentary representation came to be presented by liberal political science as the touchstone of democracy, in contrast to the diverse strains of "totalitarianism" that sought to incarnate the organic unity of the community in a mythical "people's people": the nation, the race, the class. Here we can try to complete and actualize the propositions advanced in the preceding chapters. For example, the goal of Pierre Rosanvallon's work was to systematically examine the presuppositions and limits of how the above postulate was applied, specifically in the French case, without putting the postulate itself in question (Rosanvallon, 2008). This ultimately led him to attempt to incorporate all of the forms of "counter-democracy," founded on the direct participation of citizens in administration and decision-making, into parliamentary democracy (which is fundamentally incomplete), as corrective mechanisms compensating for the "distrust" of citizens (or parliamentary democracy's loss of legitimacy). Theoreticians such as Yves Sintomer (2007) or James Holston (2008) took the exact opposite approach. Using examples from both the "South" and the "North" (the "citizen juries" of Berlin, the "participatory budgets" of Porto Alegre, the "squatter settlements" of São Paulo), they explored concrete channels of "insurgent citizenship," of which the representative institution is only one pole, albeit an indispensable one. But it was as a mechanism for expropriating the direct political capacity of citizens (their general competence, their right to expression, their capacity for decision-making: everything that Aristotle called the "general office" of citizens) that "representation" itself was criticized by communism and anarchism.

Yet there is nothing new about the crisis of parliamentarianism, and some of its symptoms are as old as its constitution – particularly the corruption of the "people's representatives," who wind up becoming intermediaries between their constituents, economic interest groups, administrators, and state power-holders, or the anti-parliamentarian reactions, which are deemed "populist," provoked by this corruption. Reading about the recent expenses scandal in the UK parliament, one thinks back to the "rotten boroughs" of eighteenth-century English parliamentary history. Or when we learn that French political parties on both the right and the left were financed by "retro-commissions" from arms trafficking and oil money from Africa and Southeast Asia, we might recall the Panama affair of 1892.

Far more interesting, from the perspective of the antinomies of citizenship, would be a discussion of the *crisis of representation as such*, beyond the parliamentary mechanism, as a collective capacity of citizens to *delegate their power* to representatives at each level where there is a need for a public office (what the ancients called a "magistrature"), and to *control the results* of this delegation. This is one of the fundamental rights of "free and equal citizens," which were invented or generalized by modernity via the "bourgeois" revolutions (Urbinati, 2006). In other words, we must return with a democratic perspective, which is to say, *from below*, to the fundamental question that Hobbes asked at the dawn of modern political philosophy *from above*, from the perspective of a complete identification between the "public sphere" (the commonwealth) and "sovereign power": what is the procedure through which the collective *acquires* power through its *transfer*, or its *communication*? This brings us back, once again, to the dialectic of "constituent power" and "constituted power," of insurrection and constitution. This time, however, we are looking for it beyond the state or *in the absence* of the state's political monopoly, rather than as its foundation. We cannot attach any a priori internal limit or boundary to this dialectic that puts the postulate of "popular ignorance" fundamentally into question. A population that is not satisfied with simply electing its representatives, but in effect controls them, will necessarily be the repository of a competency, rather than just opinion. We should be careful not to forget that in the republican tradition, teachers, police officers, and judges, whether state employees or not, are just as much "representatives of the people" as congresspersons, so long as the modalities of their selection and the effects of their actions are subject to democratic control (which, we must admit, is very unevenly the case). But representation of this kind can only become part of a "constitution of citizenship" if, on their side, the citizenry as a multitude have a real capacity to deliberate over and judge the actions of officeholders.

The crisis in the political institution designated by the general term "de-democratization" therefore resides not only in the devalorization of some *specific* form of representation, but also in the disqualification of *the very principle of representation itself.* This is because, on one side, it is assumed that this has become useless, "irrational," given the emergence of forms of "governance" that would allow us to calculate and optimize social programs and procedures for reducing conflict as a function of their utility. And, on the other, we now hear more than ever that representation is an impractical, dangerous form of politics, that the responsibility of "citizen-subjects" is defined first and foremost in terms of conforming to social norms and of deviance that must be controlled, but absolutely not expressed nor allowed to express itself by being given a "voice" (which means that the "hatred of representation" is also a form of "hatred of democracy"). Neo-liberal governance is not interested in "conflict reduction" *as such.* On the contrary, it tends to relegate conflict to zones that are "sacrificed" because they are (momentarily) "unexploitable," places where "disposable people" are kept separate (Ogilvie, 2012). Rather than reducing conflict, neo-liberalism tends to instrumentalize it, therefore exacerbating it in certain "zones," and disqualifying it through repression in others. In the end, it is simultaneously "particularized" and "repressed," and in any event violently stripped of its constituent role, which had once allowed for the access of all antagonisms and their bearers into the public sphere.

8

Democratizing Democracy

Over the course of this book, I have occasionally used the expression the "democratization of democracy." In the present day, this idea is championed by theorists as different as the advocates of a "third way" between liberalism and socialism (e.g. Anthony Giddens, Ulrich Beck) and the standard-bearers of "alter-globalization" (e.g. Boaventura de Sousa Santos). But this idea has far more ancient origins, and it can designate the movement that, by regrouping the "insurrectional" origins of citizenship (the indefinite office of the people, the principle of equaliberty, demands for "the right to rights" in the face of exclusion in its various forms, the "tribunal role" of conflicts and struggles, etc.), can give them institutional form. This expression is also used as the generic name for active resistance to the ongoing processes of "de-democratization," which are a way of closing off the history of citizenship and the "concept of the political" that it designates. We have now reached the point where, by way of a conclusion, we must attempt to synthesize this perspective.

To begin with, let us return to our original question: why argue that the ideas of citizenship and democracy are closely interrelated, given that their relationship seems to lead only to insoluble problems? And hasn't this paradox been magnified now that the term "democracy" has been rendered completely banal, serving to encompass nearly all internal and external politics (perhaps even all "policing"), particularly the erosion of the "capacities" and "virtues" traditionally associated with the historical figure of the "citizen"? Should we join this linguistic consensus, in the name of "true" democracy, or of an "essence" of democracy that would have to be excavated out from under its perversions and distortions? Will we have to smuggle in another category (such as socialism, or even communism, but also perhaps populism or nationalism) under the cover of a dominant terminology that has supplanted all the names for emancipation and resistance to established order? Or, on the contrary, should we try to upend the prevailing understanding? These questions are all worth asking, and the propositions that I advance in this conclusion also take the form of an experimentation with the meaning of words and the scope of their usage. The situation becomes more complicated still if we recognize, as we did above, that some of the crucial problems for democracy (specifically the fluctuating "distance" between pluralism and conflict) are shared by the liberal tradition and that, as a result, we cannot draw a strict line between "democratic" and "liberal" civic attitudes.

It is true that, today, a critique of established order focused specifically on the concentration of power in the hands of a financial oligarchy might have very good reasons for defending liberalism, or for showing that the prevailing usage of liberalism as a reference point in the present day is in almost complete opposition to the objectives of its classical theorists (whether it be Tocqueville, Mill, or even Montesquieu and Weber). Today, we can observe a "securitarian" or "authoritarian turn" taking place in the functioning of regimes that present themselves as liberal democracies. This has had an impact on both the exercise of civil rights and the limits of pluralism, which had earlier represented liberalism's points of pride as an "open society" (Popper, 1945). Take, for example, the exceptional laws and procedures established in the United States post-9/11, or the generalized restrictions on the right to free movement, the "manufacture" of "illegal" populations on the basis of the migration of populations (Dal Lago, 2009). Not only that, but the major themes of social and political conservatism (such as Foucault's "dangerous individual") are currently in the process of being re-established at the core of official liberalism in the name of "defending society" against a "proliferation of threats." This has led to the conflation of the categories of the delinquent and the rebel with that of the dissident. Similarly, pluralism has been put into question in the name of its own defense, particularly in the areas of "culture" and "religion," often by reactivating the old idea according to which liberty should not come to the aid of "enemies of liberty." Quite a number of the critical ideologies of history (specifically Marxism) have been demonized. But, above all, ever since Samuel Huntington (1996) discovered that the seemingly concilia-tory watchword of "multiculturalism" actually encompassed a "clash of civilizations" that threatened to destroy the Western values of individual freedom, a number of "univer-sal religions" (particularly Islam) have become a priori excluded from the range of tolerable opinions in the public space (and a fortiori excluded as legitimate sources of politi-cal engagement). This rise in intolerance is naturally global, and the West is not unique in this respect, but it is the West that purports to offer the model for democratic society.

Thus, the crisis of liberalism (which is happy to present itself, as we have seen, as the emergence of neo-liberalism) does not lead us away from reflections on the relationship of citizenship and democracy; on the contrary, it draws us back to them directly. But it suggests that it would be better for us to place them within a "strategic" perspective, rather than an essentializing "constitutional" perspective, in line with the old tradition of creating typologies of political "regimes," which started with Plato and Aristotle and today has shifted over to the opposition between democracy and totalitarianism. Here, the word "strategic" does not imply a ruse, a rhetorical shift, or simply turning categories against their dominant usage (which had, to a certain extent, been the case with the Marxist tradition when it spoke of the "conquest of democracy"), but rather an attempt to understand the significance of the continual displacement of the institutional reference points for the term "democracy." It is therefore an attempt to compel the dominant usage of this term to evolve, by taking seriously the historical alternatives that it covers. One need not believe in an eternal "essence" of citizenship whose form would have been "invented" once and for all by the ancient politeia, or the "revolution of the Rights of Man," nor maintain that there has been a guiding thread running from one usage to the next, or a link between the movements for the "democratization of democracy" emerging today (such as the Spanish "indignados," the "Arab Spring," and Occupy Wall Street) and the "traces" left by past, perhaps even ancient, insurrections. In one sense, these past insurrections constitute symbolic forces that "overdetermine" the material forces underlying current situations (particularly social situations). This is why abandoning the terms "democracy" and "citizenship" would not be a renewal of the political, so much as it would be resigning in the face of the difficult task that confronts the political today: finding forms of collective autonomy that would correspond to the environment of globalization. On this point, we can agree with Rancière (2006), who demonstrated the indissoluble nature of the relationship between the "concept of the political" and the "concept of democracy." But we should also distinguish ourselves from him (or incorporate his radically egalitarian intuitions into a more dialectical framework) by pointing out that the anti-political (which he,

playing skillfully with etymology, calls by the name "police")
is not a reality that is foreign to the political (and therefore
to democracy) but a *counter-tendency* that is internal to it,
and from which the political is constantly seeking to disassociate and differentiate itself. It is the reality of this internal
conflict, whose forms are continually evolving, that from our
perspective justifies the recourse to "citizenship" in addition
to democracy, or, better yet, in close conjunction with it.

In many respects the terminological problem we face here
is the same as the one Marx pondered (and that gave him
pause) during the crucial period of his "critique of the political" (in the period spanning from the *Critique of Hegel's
"Philosophy of Right"* of 1843 to the *Communist Manifesto*
of 1848), between the idea of a *political conflict* (or a class
struggle), which would correspond to the "conquest of
democracy," and the idea of an essentially "apolitical" social
movement, which would "put an end to the political state"
as a power that is "separate" from the activities and demands
of the population or the *demos*. Here we find something that
is, it would seem, analogous to the *dissymmetry* of conflict
and that also relates to both the exercise of power and the
form of institutions, whose importance to Machiavelli and
his modern-day interpreters we have already emphasized.

All of this leads us to "strategically" incorporate into the
idea of the "democratization of democracy" a dimension of
reflexive citizenship – reflecting on the struggles of its own
history. It would thus acquire the validity of a full-fledged
"concept of the political," but on the condition of distin-
guishing it from other contemporary uses of this expression,
which make it into a "third way" or a compromise arrange-
ment between revolutionary transformation and the established order of property and representation. This is why we
will attempt to characterize a critical conception of citizenship founded on this formulation through the means of seven
"theses" or theoretical propositions.

Proposition 1 The democratization of democracy designates *neither* a process for perfecting an existing "democratic" regime *nor* a state that virtually "transcends" any possible regime – in the way that, for example, Derrida (2005) described democracy as "always to come," making it synonymous with unconditional justice, for which we would have expectations that would exceed any legal or institutional possibility. But it does designate a *difference* with regard to current practices of the political, or, better yet, a "differential" that displaces political practices in such a way as to openly confront the *lack of democracy* in existing institutions and transform them in a more or less radical manner. The active citizen is the agent of this transformation. This is why she always retains a connection to the ideas of insurrection and revolution, not only in the sense of a simple "event," whether violent or non-violent, that would interrupt institutional continuity, but also in the sense of a process that is continually begun anew, whose forms and objectives would vary depending on shifting historical conditions.

Proposition 2 Without a permanent transformation of this kind, there is no true democracy *as such*, except as memory, myth, or propaganda tool. But a transformation of this kind must, for its part, *transgress* limits and recognized institutional forms. It must, to borrow Claude Lefort's (1981) formulation, involve a "democratic invention." There is therefore no status quo when it comes to citizenship: either it "advances," which is to say, it articulates *new fundamental rights*, which are both "rights of man" and "rights of the citizen," and develops them with varying degrees of speed into institutions (such as social security, the right to work, citizenship for foreigners, etc.), or it "regresses," which means that it loses the rights it had acquired (including the "rights of man"), or that these rights are transformed into their opposites, via different "anti-political" modalities, be they authoritarian, bureaucratic, discriminatory, or paternalistic. This is a necessary precondition materially as well as ideologically, and it has a bearing upon the secret relationship between power apparatuses and mass ideologies (ranging from populism to voluntary servitude), as well as the back and forth between the politicization and de-politicization of citizenship. This means that a constitutional measure only has "civic" content to the extent that it creates *more rights* and *more participation* or a greater *representation* of the interests and opinions of citizens than the measure that it replaces. Contemporary Europe offers a dramatic illustration of the importance of this requirement. But this also means that democracy, insofar as it is identified with its own continuous democratization, requires the deconstruction of the discriminations and exclusions that have been institutionalized in its name (here again, the example of women and foreigners is of particular importance).

Such is the problem that confronts the "new social movements" of every era, which go unrecognized or fluctuate between the "private" and "public" sphere. It is also the yardstick against which we should measure "old social movements" (in our time, these would be labor unions, and organizations of the labor movement in general), which are fighting to defend a threatened form of democratic citizenship (social citizenship, and its correlates in terms of universal social protection or the right to employment, which "politicize" the social as much as they "socialize" the political). More fundamentally still, this is the problem involved in the transformation of *national borders* in a democratic sense (i.e. specifically in the way that it allows for a *circulation* of political projects and actors between territories), and therefore the transcendence of purely national sovereignty, not only as state sovereignty, but as sovereignty "of the people." It is unnecessary to once again emphasize at length how important this kind of transgression of territorial and

communal fences is when it comes to bringing into the field
of the political (and not only of "governance") urgent global
questions such as the environment, migrations, the usage of
"common" resources, the prevention of ethnic conflicts, and
so on.

Proposition 3   The common lesson of the first two propositions could be summarized by returning to a formulation
that emerged out of social democratic debates of the nineteenth century, one that was rejected simultaneously by the
adherents of both liberalism and revolutionary Marxism.
Eduard Bernstein (the father of Marxist "revisionism")
advanced this idea in his 1899 book *The Preconditions of
Socialism* (*Die Voraussetzungen des Sozialismus und die
Aufgaben der Sozialdemokratie*) in the form: "This goal [the
final goal of socialism], whatever it may be, is nothing to
me, the movement is everything" (Bernstein, 1993 [1899]:
xxvii). This thesis was not without its similarities to the
idea of a "permanent revolution" that Marx momentarily
defended in the years immediately following the democratic
(national and socialist) revolutions of 1848 and their failure,
from which he hoped the European people would quickly
recover.
    Bernstein was not, strictly speaking, a "reformist," in the
sense of someone trying to find a compromise with capitalism (at least, no more so than Lenin was during the period
of the "New Economic Policy"). Rather, he was a theorist
of the *transformation of the power struggle* between the
classes. His formulation is important here because it draws
a link between the question of the effective *threshold of
transformation* of a given social and political regime, and
the effective threshold for the *uniting of struggles* for democracy and against capitalism (which Gramsci would later
call a hegemony, owing to its ideological form). This suggests that we should take into consideration the historically ambiguous relationship between the development of

capitalism and the development of citizenship in some areas
of the world (and perhaps over time in all of them, in various
forms: Chatterjee, 2004), but also the more radical idea that
capitalism can be compelled into incorporating rights that
contradict its own logic. The key is knowing whether such
a transformation of the power struggle can reach a point
where it begins to make room for non-commercial relationships that are neither residual nor compensatory (such as the
recent neo-liberal philanthropy) but expansive. Even if these
are not little islands of communism in the ancient sense
of "modes of production" that organize the totality of
the society (and abolish the political), then they might at
least be what Hardt and Negri (2009) called "commons"
(not only "common goods," but "community practices").
This comes down to incorporating an element of the critique
of capitalism, derived from the Marxist tradition, into the
problematic of citizenship, but doing so by *inverting* the way
in which it is inserted into the course of historical transformations, changing its status from that of a "result" to that
of a "means," or, better yet, a "motive force." We might be
tempted to introduce the idea of a "revolution in the revolution," which Régis Debray (1990 [1967]) employed to characterize the Cuban Revolution at the time when it seemed to
promise the return of liberation struggles in Latin America.

Proposition 4   A democratization of democracy therefore
involves, in a strict sense, giving priority to the positive
objective of transforming the concept and practices of citizenship, of "democratic invention," over the negative objective of resistance and opposition to non-democratic laws or
regimes. But this does not mean, of course, that it could
occur without regime change or power struggles that push
the phenomena of "de-democratization" into retreat. To put
it better: paradoxically, it is always the inventive, affirmative element (a new conception of citizenship, a change in
the modalities of individual and collective struggles that

constitute political *activity*) that conditions the negative element, the capacity to resist anti-democratic politics and institutional attacks on equal rights and freedoms. Here we can find the fundamental lessons of the insurrectional movements of 1968 across the world (which have often been obscured by both their critics and their participants), which we might attempt to elaborate as follows:

- No society or state can import democracy from the outside. It is created or re-created on the basis of political practices or – to use Engin Isin and Greg Nielsen's (2008) expression – "acts of citizenship" that grant it material existence. Nevertheless, "exceptional" historical circumstances (wars, economic crises, defeats, the overthrow of dictatorships or totalitarian regimes, etc.) represent *negative conditions* in which the urgency of acts of citizenship is felt more vividly, and their contrast with "passive citizenship," or passivity without citizenship, becomes more conspicuous.

- The democratic transformation of a society or economic system (such as capitalism) via means or procedures that are themselves non-democratic, or even anti-democratic, is radically impossible. This is the lesson of the tragic history of communism and socialism in the twentieth century (and therefore of the debates over the "dictatorship of the proletariat," in which political conflict was *made symmetrical* once again through theory and organizational practice that established a "counter-state" to oppose the "state"), as well as the anti-imperialist national liberation movements. We must return to the idea that a force or a political movement can only democratize society if it itself is fundamentally *more democratic* than the system it opposes, with respect both to its objectives and to its internal operation.

- While this formulation might appear to be purely *negative*, given its historical references, it is in fact fundamentally positive or "affirmative," because it implies that a struggle for democracy is at the same time an *experience of democratic citizenship*, an attempt to expand the spaces of liberty and equality. This is an essential dimension of past "insurrectional" movements or "revolutionary" processes that has been retrieved by the current struggles of different "subaltern" groups; their empowerment reflects not only the reversal of an external power struggle, but also the internal ability of the militants involved to free themselves from the shackles of discipline and to offer a prefiguration of an egalitarian community of citizens that is deliberative, decisive, and action-taking.

Proposition 5 A democratization of democracy therefore not only refers to the transformation of institutions, structures, and relationships of power. It is also the name we could give to the *work citizens perform* upon themselves in a given historical situation. It aims to overcome both the external, or "objective," and internal, or "subjective," obstacles to action and political participation. Even Marx recognized this dimension of emancipation when, following the failure of the 1848 revolutions, he explained in his private correspondence that the workers needed time in order to "educate themselves about the revolution" that they wished to create. This process might seem circular, or at least enigmatic. In Foucault's (1982) terminology, it corresponds to the passage from *subjection* to *subjectivation*, as a modality of "self-government," which need not necessarily remain purely individualistic. In the final analysis, it implies an exit from "voluntary servitude," which La Boétie (2012 [1576]) contrasted with republican government, turning the Platonic critique of tyranny back against its initial aim. Voluntary servitude can be caused by *fear*, which is undoubtedly one of its most powerful tools – here we can think back to Hobbes' (1981 [1651]) description of the terror and awe inspired by the disproportionate power of the sovereign. But then, there is always the risk that this fear might turn into revolt. It can be induced by *ideology*, ranging from the influence of education to the propaganda apparatuses and media that shape public opinion. Lastly, it can be the result of *freedom* itself, or, rather, of certain uses of freedom that detach the individual from the conditions of her own action, on the model of Marx's description of the "freedom" of the wage laborer, which we could argue extends to all the effects of individualism in contemporary politics. These are accentuated by the fact that they cannot be separated from mass conformity, which is upheld by the reign of consumption and the corporate media (as the Frankfurt School theorists maintained from the very start).

It is this intrinsically conflictual relationship between democracy and voluntary servitude that explains why so many theorists have made *civic disobedience* one of the fundamental criteria of the "virtue" of the citizen – contingent on an understanding and appreciation of the circumstances, of course; because civil disobedience has *both* the ability to regenerate political activity and the ability to annihilate it, in an antinomic manner, particularly when it transitions (as Hannah Arendt [1972] indicated) from the exercise of an individual "right" to a "strategy" of collective resistance to tyranny.

Proposition 6 A democratization of democracy is therefore essentially a struggle on several fronts, or, to use less military imagery, it is an activity that takes place on several "stages" simultaneously. The value of an analysis of citizenship of the kind advanced here, which successively brings into play insurrection, the conquest of social citizenship, and the aporias of the institution of conflict, is that it can suggest an intertwining of several movements whose convergence is not automatic: movements for "active" citizenship, political participation, and the abolition of exclusion, whether it be the exclusion of the poor or exclusions focused on anthropological differences; "counter-democracy" movements (Rosanvallon, 2008), or, better yet, movements to counter the anti-democratic effects of the monopoly of expertise and representation; and, finally, movements that tend to transform into open conflict (and as such into demands for *recognition*) the resistance and demands for justice by social groups that are being "excluded from the distribution of power" because of its monopolistic character. All of these movements, whether they are based on class condition or the contestation of other relationships of domination, are thus only "constituent" insofar as they are also "insurgent." In a certain sense they act as the opposite of the "constitutional guarantees" upon which liberalism always insists, because they attempt to ward off the inherent risks of popular "sovereignty" that would be *overly limited*, rather than excessive.

From which we get the following recapitulative proposition:

Proposition 7 Insurrection, in its *different* forms, is the active modality of citizenship: the modality that it brings into *action*. We can then say that the "final result" is in fact a function of the "movement," which is the true modality of the existence of the political. But we must not think that there is a "correct midpoint" between insurrection and de-democratization, or the decomposition of the political. Insurrection is called "the conquest of democracy" or "the right to have rights," but its content is always the search for (or the risk of) collective emancipation and the power that it bestows upon its participants – in contrast to established order, which tends to suppress this power. Our current moment in the history of the institutions of citizenship offers an eloquent illustration of how radical this alternative is as well as the uncertainty involved.

References

Abensour, Miguel (2006) *Hannah Arendt contre la philosophie politique?* Paris: Sens & Tonka.

Agamben, Giorgio (2004) "Non au tatouage biopolitique," *Le Monde diplomatique*, 10 January.

Agamben, Giorgio (2005) *State of Exception*, trans. Kevin Attell. Chicago: University of Chicago Press.

Anderson, Benedict (1983) *Imagined Communities*. London: Verso.

Arendt, Hannah (1951) *The Origins of Totalitarianism*. New York: Harcourt, Brace and Company.

Arendt, Hannah (1972) "On Civil Disobedience," in *Crises of the Republic*. New York: Harcourt Brace Jovanovich.

Aristotle (2009) *The Politics*, trans. Ernest Barker, intro. R.F. Stalley. Oxford and New York: Oxford University Press.

Aron, Raymond (1965) *Democracy and Totalitarianism*, trans. Valence Ionescu. London: Weidenfeld & Nicolson.

Balibar, Étienne (2013) *Equaliberty: Political Essays*, trans. James Ingram. Durham, NC: Duke University Press.

Baudrillard, Jean (1994) *Simulacra and Simulation*, trans. Sheila Faria Glaser. Ann Arbor: University of Michigan Press.

Bauman, Zygmunt (1999) *In Search of Politics*. Cambridge: Polity.

Benveniste, Émile (1974) "Deux modèles linguistiques de la cité," in *Problèmes de linguistique générale*, II. Paris: Gallimard.

Bernstein, Eduard (1993 [1899]) *The Preconditions of Socialism*, trans. Henry Tudor. Cambridge: Cambridge University Press.

Body-Gendrot, Sophie (2001) *Les villes – La fin de la violence?* Paris: Presses de Sciences Po.

Brown, Wendy (2003) "Neo-Liberalism and the End of Liberal Democracy," *Theory and Event*, 7:1, 1–29.

Caloz-Tschopp, Marie-Claire (2004) *Les étrangers aux frontières de l'Europe et le spectre des camps*. Paris: La Dispute.

Cassin, Barbara, ed. (2014) *Dictionary of Untranslatables: A Philosophical Lexicon*, eds Emily Apter, Jacques Lezra, and Michael Wood, trans. Steven Rendall, Christian Hubert, Jeffrey Mehlman, Nathaniel Stein, and Michael Syrotinski. Princeton: Princeton University Press.

Castel, Robert (2003) *From Manual Workers to Wage Laborers: Transformation of the Social Question*, trans. and ed. Richard Boyd. New Brunswick, NJ: Transaction Publishers.

Castel, Robert (2007) *La Discrimination négative: citoyens ou indigènes?* Paris: Éditions du Seuil.

Castel, Robert (2009) *La montée des incertitudes: travail, protections, statut de l'individu*. Paris: Seuil.

Chatterjee, Partha (2004) *The Politics of the Governed: Reflections on Popular Politics in Most of the World*. New York: Columbia University Press.

Cicero, Marcus Tullius (2008) *The Republic and the Laws*, trans. Niall Rudd, intro. Jonathan Powell and Niall Rudd. Oxford: Oxford University Press.

Cohen, Jean and Andrew Arato (1992) *Civil Society and Political Theory*. Cambridge, MA: MIT Press.

Colliot-Thélène, Catherine (2011) *La démocratie sans "demos."* Paris: Presses Universitaires de France.

Dal Lago, Alessandro (2009) *Non-Persons: The Exclusion of Migrants in a Global Society*, trans. Marie Orton. Milan: IPOC.

de Brunhoff, Suzanne (1986) *L'heure du marché: critique du libéralisme*. Paris: Presses Universitaires de France.

de Sousa Santos, Boaventura (2005) "General Introduction. Reinventing Social Emancipation: Toward New Manifestos," in *Democratizing Democracy: Beyond the Liberal Democratic Canon*. London and New York: Verso.

Debray, Régis (1990 [1967]) *Revolution in the Revolution*, trans. Bobbye Ortiz. New York: Grove Press.

Deleuze, Gilles (1990) "Societies of Control," in *Negotiations*, trans. Martin Joughin. New York: Columbia University Press.

Deleuze, Gilles and Félix Guattari (1987) *A Thousand Plateaus: Capitalism and Schizophrenia*, trans. Brian Massumi. Minneapolis and London: University of Minnesota Press.

Derrida, Jacques (2005) *Rogues: Two Essays on Reason*, trans. Pascale-Anne Brault and Michael Naas. Stanford: Stanford University Press.

Esposito, Roberto (1993) *Nove pensieri sulla politica*. Bologna: Il Mulino.

Essed, Philomena (2005) "Racisme et préférence pour l'identique: du clonage culturelle dans la vie quotidienne," *Revue Marx Actuel* 38: *Le Racisme après les races*: 103–18.

Fichte, Johann Gottlieb (1973 [1795]) *Beiträge zur Berichtigung der Urteil des Publikums über die französische Revolution*. Hamburg: Felix Meiner.

Fichte, Johann Gottlieb (2008 [1808]) *Addresses to the German Nation*, trans. Gregory Moore. Cambridge: Cambridge University Press.

Foucault, Michel (1975) *Discipline and Punish: The Birth of the Prison*, trans. Alan Sheridan. London: Penguin.

Foucault, Michel (1982) "The Subject and Power," trans. Leslie Sawyer, *Critical Inquiry*, 8:4, 777–95.

Foucault, Michel (2003a) *Abnormal: Lectures at the Collège de France, 1974–1975*, trans. Graham Burchell. New York: Picador.

Foucault, Michel (2003b) *Society Must Be Defended: Lectures at the Collège de France, 1975–1976*, trans. David Macey. New York: Picador.

Foucault, Michel (2008) *The Birth of Biopolitics: Lectures at the Collège de France, 1978–1979*, trans. Graham Burchell. New York and Basingstoke: Palgrave Macmillan.

Fraisse, Geneviève (2001) *Les deux gouvernements: la famille et la cité*. Paris: Gallimard.

Fukuyama, Francis (1992) *The End of History and the Last Man*. New York: Free Press.

Gaille-Nikodimov, Marie (2004) *Conflit civil et liberté: la politique machiavélienne entre histoire et médecine*. Paris: Champion.

Galli, Carlo (2010) *Political Spaces and Global War*, ed. Adam Sitze, trans. Elisabeth Fay. Minneapolis: University of Minnesota Press.

Gauthier, Florence (1998) *Triomphe et mort du droit naturel en Révolution*. Paris: Presses Universitaires de France.

Gramsci, Antonio (1992) *Prison Notebooks*, ed. Joseph A. Buttigieg, trans. Joseph A. Buttigieg and Antonio Callari. New York: Cambridge University Press.

Habermas, Jürgen (1984) *The Theory of Communicative Action*, Vol. 1: *Reason and the Rationalization of Society*, trans. Thomas McCarthy. Boston: Beacon.

Habermas, Jürgen (1989) *The Structual Transformation of the Public Sphere: An Inquiry into a Category of Bourgeois Society*, trans. Thomas Burger and Frederick Lawrence. Cambridge, MA: MIT Press.

Hardt, Michael and Antonio Negri (2000) *Empire*. Cambridge, MA: Harvard University Press.

Hardt, Michael and Antonio Negri (2004) *Multitude: War and Democracy in the Age of Empire*. New York: Penguin.

Hardt, Michael and Antonio Negri (2009) *Commonwealth*. Cambridge, MA: Belknap Press of Harvard University Press.

Hayek, Friedrich (1944) *The Road to Serfdom*. London: Routledge.

Hegel, Georg Wilhelm Friedrich (1991 [1820]) *Elements of the Philosophy of Right*, ed. Allen Wood, trans. H.B. Nisbet. Cambridge: Cambridge University Press.

Hobbes, Thomas (1981 [1651]) *Leviathan*, ed. C. MacPherson. Harmondsworth: Penguin.

Holston, James (2008) *Insurgent Citizenship: Disjunctions of Democracy and Modernity in Brazil*. Princeton: Princeton University Press.

Horkheimer, Max and Theodor W. Adorno (1972 [1944]) *Dialectic of Enlightenment*, trans. John Cumming. New York: Herder and Herder.

Huntington, Samuel (1996) *The Clash of Civilizations and the Remaking of World Order*. New York: Simon & Schuster.

Isin, Engin F. and Greg M. Nielsen (2008) *Acts of Citizenship*. London: Zed Books.

Kant, Immanuel (1983 [1796]) *Perpetual Peace and Other Essays*, trans. Ted Humphrey, Indianapolis, IN: Hackett.

Kant, Immanuel (2006 [1798]) *Anthropology from a Pragmatic Point of View*, trans. and ed. Robert B. Louden. Cambridge: Cambridge University Press.

Kelsen, Hans (2013) *The Essence and Value of Democracy*, eds Nadia Urbinati and Carlo Invernizzi Accetti, trans. Brian Graf. Lanham, MD: Rowman & Littlefield Publishers.

Kymlicka, Will (1995) *Multicultural Citizenship: A Liberal Theory of Minority Rights*. Oxford: Oxford University Press.

La Boétie, Étienne de (2012 [1576]) *Discourse on Voluntary Servitude*, trans. James B. Atkinson and David Sices, intro. James B. Atkinson. Indianapolis, IN: Hackett.

Laclau, Ernesto (2002) *On Populist Reason*. London: Verso.

Lavau, Georges (1981) *À quoi sert le Parti communiste français?* Paris: Fayard.

Lefort, Claude (1981) *L'invention démocratique*. Paris: Fayard.

Leggewie, Claus (1990) *Multi Kulti: Spielregeln fur die Vielvolkerrepublik*. Berlin: Rotbuch Verlag.

Lemke, Thomas (2001) "The Birth of Bio-Politics: Michel Foucault's Lecture at the Collège de France on Neo-Liberal Governmentality," *Economy and Society*, 30:2, 190–207.

Loraux, Nicole (2006) *The Divided City: On Memory and Forgetting in Ancient Athens*, trans. Corinne Pacha and Jeff Fort. New York: Zone Books.

Lordon, Frédéric (2008) *Jusqu'à quand? Pour en finir avec les crises financières*. Paris: Éditions Raisons d'agir.

Machiavelli, Niccolò (1996 [1531]) *Discourses on Livy*, trans. Harvey C. Mansfield and Nathan Tarcov. Chicago: University of Chicago Press.

Marcuse, Herbert (1964) *One-Dimensional Man: Studies in the Ideology of Advanced Industrial Society*. London: Abacus.

Marramo, Giacomo (1995) *Dopo il Leviatano*. Turin: Giappichelli.

Marshall, T.H. (1950) *Citizenship and Social Class*. London: Cambridge University Press.

Marx, Karl (1970 [1843]) *Critique of Hegel's "Philosophy of Right,"* trans. Annette Jolin and Joseph O'Malley, intro. Joseph O'Malley. Cambridge: Cambridge University Press.

Marx, Karl (1992 [1867]) *Capital: Volume 1: A Critique of Political Economy*, trans. Ben Fowkes, intro. Ernest Mandel. Harmondsworth: Penguin.

Marx, Karl (2005 [1852]) *The Eighteenth Brumaire of Louis Bonaparte*, trans. Daniel de Leon. New York: Mondial.

Mezzadra, Sandro (2001) *Diritto di fuga: migrazioni, cittadinanza, globalizzazione*. Verona: Ombre Corte.

Michels, Robert (1915) *Political Parties: A Sociological Study of the Oligarchical Tendencies of Modern Democracies*, trans. Eden and Cedar Paul. London: Jarrold & Sons.

Mortati, Costantino (1940) *La costituzione in senso materiale.* Milan: Giuffrè.

Mouffe, Chantal (2000) *The Democratic Paradox.* London: Verso.

Muehlebach, Andrea (2012) *The Moral Neoliberal: Welfare and Citizenship in Italy.* Chicago: University of Chicago Press.

Nancy, Jean-Luc (1990) *The Inoperative Community,* trans. Peter Connor et al., intro. Christopher Fynsk. Minneapolis and London: University of Minnesota Press.

Negri, Antonio (1999) *Insurgencies: Constituent Power and the Modern State,* trans. Maurizia Boscagli. Minneapolis: University of Minnesota Press.

Negt, Oskar and Alexander Kluge (1993) *Public Sphere and Experience: Toward an Analysis of the Bourgeois and Proletarian Public Sphere,* trans. Peter Labanyi, Jamie Owen Daniel, and Assenka Oksiloff, intro. Miriam Hansen. Minneapolis: University of Minnesota Press.

Nietzsche, Friedrich (1978 [1885]) *Thus Spoke Zarathustra: A Book for None and All,* trans. Walter Kaufmann. New York: Penguin Press.

O'Connor, James (1973) *The Fiscal Crisis of the State.* New York: St Martin's Press.

Ogilvie, Bertrand (2012) *L'homme jetable: essai sur l'exterminisme et la violence extrême.* Paris: Éditions Amsterdam.

Pocock, J.G.A. (1975) *The Machiavellian Moment.* Princeton: Princeton University Press.

Popper, Karl (1945) *Open Society and Its Enemies.* London: Routledge.

Rancière, Jacques (1999) *Disagreement: Politics and Philosophy,* trans. Julie Rose. Minneapolis and London: University of Minnesota Press.

Rancière, Jacques (2006) *Hatred of Democracy,* trans. Steve Corcoran. London: Verso.

Rawls, John (1971) *A Theory of Justice.* Cambridge, MA: Belknap Press of Harvard University Press.

Rawls, John (1993) *Political Liberalism.* New York: Columbia University Press.

Rosanvallon, Pierre (1998) *Le Peuple introuvable: histoire de la représentation démocratique en France.* Paris: Gallimard.

Rosanvallon, Pierre (2008) *Counter-Democracy: Politics in an Age of Distrust,* trans. Arthur Goldhammer. Cambridge and New York: Cambridge University Press.

Rousseau, Jean-Jacques (1968 [1762]) *The Social Contract*, trans. Maurice Cranstone. London: Penguin.

Samaddar, Ranabir (2007) *The Materiality of Politics*, Vol. 1: *The Technologies of Rule*; Vol. 2: *Subject Positions in Politics*. London: Anthem Press.

Sassen, Saskia (2006) *Territory, Authority, Rights: From Medieval to Global Assemblages*. Princeton: Princeton University Press.

Sassoon, Donald (1996) *One Hundred Years of Socialism: The West European Left in the Twentieth Century*. New York: The New Press.

Schmitt, Carl (1976 [1932]) *The Concept of the Political*, trans. George Schwab, intro. George Schwab, comments Leo Strauss. New Brunswick, NJ: Rutgers University Press.

Schmitt, Carl (2003 [1950]) *The Nomos of the Earth in the International Law of the Jus Publicum Europaeum*, trans. G.L. Ulmen. New York: Telos Press.

Schmitt, Carl (2008 [1928]) *Constitutional Theory*, ed. and trans. Jeffrey Seitzer, intro. Ellen Kennedy. Durham, NC, and London: Duke University Press.

Sintomer, Yves (2007) *Le Pouvoir du peuple*. Paris: La Découverte.

Somers, Margaret (2008) *Genealogies of Citizenship: Markets, Statelessness, and the Right to Have Rights*. Cambridge and New York: Cambridge University Press.

Spinoza, Benedictus (2005 [1677]) *Political Treatise*, trans. Samuel Shirley, intro. Steven Barbone and Lee Rice. London: Hackett.

Spinoza, Benedictus (2007 [1672]) *Theological-Political Treatise*, ed. Jonathan Israel, trans. Jonathan Israel and Michael Silverthorne. Cambridge: Cambridge University Press.

Stourzh, Gerald (1989) *Wege zur Grundrechtsdemokratie: Studien zur Begriffs- und Institutionengeschichte des liberalen Verfassungsstaates*. Vienna: Boehlau Verlag.

Urbinati, Nadia (2006) *Representative Democracy: Principles and Genealogy*. Chicago: University of Chicago Press.

Van Gunsteren, Herman (1998) *A Theory of Citizenship: Organizing Plurality in Contemporary Democracies*. Boulder, CO: Westview.

Wacquant, Loïc (2004) *Urban Outcasts: A Comparative Sociology of Advanced Marginality*, trans. John Howe. Cambridge: Polity.

Wallerstein, Immanuel (1995) *After Liberalism*. New York: New Press.

Wallerstein, Immanuel, Giovanni Arrighi, and Terence Hopkins (1989) *Antisystemic Movements*. London: Verso.

Weber, Max (1957 [1921]) *The City*, ed. and trans. Don Martindale and Gertrud Neuwirth. Glencoe, IL: Free Press.

Weber, Max (1978 [1922]) *Economy and Society*, ed. Guenther Roth and Claus Wittich, trans. Ephraim Fishchoff et al. Berkeley: University of California Press.

Index

Caloz-Tschopp, M.-C. 66
capitalism
  material constitutions 51–5
  and social citizenship 47,
    59–61
  and socialism 55–6, 58
  see also globalization/global
    capitalism
Cassin, B. 11
Castel, R. 46, 56, 63–4, 67,
  112
Chatterjee, P. 7, 127
Cicero 29–30
city states *see* Greek concepts;
  Roman concepts
civil disobedience 130
civil society 25–8
class struggle
  democracy and 42–4
  see also displacement of
    antagonism
Cold War 54–5
collective identification
  23–4
collective/social
  movements 42–3,
  125–6
Colliot-Thélène, C. 40
commonwealth 8, 35
community of citizens
  and autonomy of the
    political 19–21
  and consensus 90
  and nationality 34–6
  and negative individualism
    112
compensatory communities
  113
conflictual democracy 83–4
  dissymmetrical relationship
    98–101

"illegitimate dominion" and
  "agonistic pluralism"
  93–8
liberalism, pluralism, and
  representation 87–93
violence and
  counter-violence 85–7
consensus
  and community of citizens
    90
  and conflict 17–18, 32–3
constitution of citizenship
  (*politeia*) 4, 7–10
  autonomy of the
    political 19–21
  and civil society 25–8
  and "invention of
    democracy" 10–18
  and "withering away of the
    state" 21–4
"constitutional" and
  "strategic"
  perspectives 121–3
constitution(s)
  insurrection and 31–3, 37,
    38
  material 51–5
  types 39–40
contingent character of
  democracy 33–4
control of individuals 110–11
cosmopolitanism 71–2, 82
"counter-democracy"
  115–18
counter-violence, violence and
  85–7

de Sousa Santos, B. 44, 106
"de-democratization" 4, 6, 37,
  104–5, 107, 108, 117–18
debt 107–8

142 *Index*

Deleuze, G. 110–11
and Guattari, F. 68
democracy
and citizenship, antinomic
relationship 1–6
and class struggle 42–4
"counter-democracy"
115–18
"invention of
democracy" 10–18
see also conflictual
democracy
democratic and national
socialism 55–8
"democratic paradox" 1, 33
democratization 119–23
propositions 124–31
Derrida, J. 10, 113, 124
discrimination and
inequalities 63–5
displacement of
antagonism 47–8, 53–5,
60–1, 92–3

educational systems
41–2
equal opportunity 59
equal rights and
liberty 15–16, 30–1, 33,
38, 43
see also inequalities
Essed, P. 85
eugenics programs 81
European Union 24
exclusion 62–3
and conflict 85, 86
inequalities and
discrimination 63–5
internal 69–70, 74, 86
political
anthropology 78–82

question of "right to
rights" 65–8, 74–5
rules of inclusion and 72–8
territoriality 68–72
external hostility, internal
solidarity and 97

Fichte, J.G. 74, 79
Foucault, M. 48, 70, 80, 94,
96, 98, 103–4, 111–12,
129
Fraisse, G. 50, 65
Fukuyama, F. 106

Galli, C. 68
Gauthier, F. 30
ghettos/*banlieues* 63–4
global organizations 27
globalization/global
capitalism 20, 21
acceleration of 53, 55
alter-globalization 44
compensatory
communities 113
and cosmopolitanism 71–2,
82
"crisis" 46
"governmentality" 98, 103–4
Gramsci, A. 10, 42, 85, 114
Greek concepts 2–3, 4, 8–18,
19–21, 95

Habermas, J. 58, 90–1
Hardt, M. and Negri,
A. 25–6, 110, 127
Hayek, F. 48, 112
Hegel, G.W.F. 29, 39, 40,
100
Hobbes, T. 40, 117, 130
Horkheimer, M. and Adorno,
T.W. 81